Blooming Marvellous

A Wildflower Hunter's Year

After ZOË DEVLIN retired,
she combined her interests in
botany and photography by developing
www.wildflowersofireland.net,
an enormously popular forum for those
interested in seeking out, identifying and
sharing wildflowers in Ireland. She writes a
monthly article for *The Irish Garden* and for
Woodland, the magazine of the Native
Woodland Trust. She regularly gives
lectures and guided walks, and was
named Distinguished Recorder of the
Year 2016 by the National
Biodiversity Data
Centre.

This book is dedicated to Sir David Attenborough who has given decades of enlightenment and inspiration to so many people and has instilled in us a love and respect for all parts of our biodiversity. With many thanks.

Blooming Marvellous

A Wildflower Hunter's Year

Zoë Devlin

The Collins Press

FIRST PUBLISHED IN 2017 by
The Collins Press
West Link Park
Doughcloyne
Wilton
Cork
T12 N5EF
Ireland

A CIP record for this book is available from the British Library.

Hardback ISBN: 978-1-84889-327-6

Design and typesetting by Studio10 Design
Typeset in Bembo
Printed in Poland by Białostockie Zakłady Graficzne SA

Photographs: page i: Meadow with Yellow-rattle and Cut-leaved Crane's-bill; page ii: Green-winged Orchid; page iii: leaves of Lesser Meadow-rue; facing page: Daisy.

CONTENTS

Yellow horned-
Poppy

introduction

Pyramidal
Orchid

WORDSWORTH HAD A WAY WITH WORDS that many have envied. In 1798, on the banks of the River Wye, that self-proclaimed 'worshipper of nature' wrote 'Nature never did betray the heart that loved her.' Long before I ever knew those words, my less eloquent maxim was 'Nature never, ever lets you down.' Either way, I think nature lovers will agree with both sentiments.

I was a 'war baby', growing up in Dublin in the middle of the last century, lucky enough to live in a suburb where there were meadows and a stream close by. These provided a backdrop to my early days, a bond with nature that I took for granted – green-tinted glasses through which I viewed much of my life.

I have had a love affair with nature for as long as I can remember. What seemed at first to be a casual awareness grew into a worthwhile pastime, then a regular hobby, and over the last few decades it has become an enduring passion. My particular focus, within the natural world, was always wildflowers, and specifically those found in Ireland.

In 2009, when I retired, I created the website www.wildflowersofireland. net. This was to be the start of a two-way dialogue with so many other interested people, in Ireland and abroad, about our native and introduced wildflowers, where they might be found, when they bloom, the place they occupy in our folklore, their role in herbal medicine and how they have been depicted in literature and art. It has also made me many good friends.

This passion for wildflowers sometimes borders on what others might term 'insanity'. I am not alone. There is a small band of obsessives who, like me, could bore others to death on the subject. My intention in this book is not to bore, but instead to share with you some of the stories connecting me to certain species of wildflowers. Some of them relate to the place where I found a particular species, some to the people who were with me at the time. Others tell of the history of the location where the wildflower grew and then there are some which tell a little about my own life, which could be, admittedly on occasion, somewhat bizarre. I have also written about the family members who encouraged and supported me in my desire to learn more about wildflowers and botany and to whom I owe a great debt of gratitude.

The book has been divided into twelve chapters, connecting the flowering time of each species to its own story. My suggestion to readers is to pick it up and open it on a page of the current month. Perhaps you will find one of the flowers featured and have a story to tell me in return.

Yellow Iris

Eanáir
january

After Janus, god of beginnings,
transitions and doors. The first
month of the year in both Julian and
Gregorian calendars • Second month
of winter in Ireland

Groundsel

Most people might imagine that a wildflower lover's year never starts until spring, but this is not the case. In fact, it starts when winter still has us in her cold, steely grip – as well as our thermal underwear.

Poring over wildflower books, county floras and last year's notes and records, there is a growing sense of anticipation. Each of us has our own holy grail and, while I don't admit to being a 'twitcher', I have been known to travel certain roads at certain times of the year, just in case. Hope springs eternal in an amateur botanist's breast. Perhaps when they vaccinated me as a baby, someone put sap into the syringe … it was enough to get me hooked on plants for life. Every January I get a visceral, primeval feeling and there is nothing I can do about it – even if I wanted to.

Sitting by the fire in this, the middle month of winter, my spirits always lift. Reading my scribbled accounts from previous years brings back some of the knowledge gained but more often forgotten. It stirs up a warm sense of optimism for what I might find this year, if I'm lucky. Occasionally, when I get out for a walk, I play the game of guessing 'What is that plant going to be when it grows up?' Trying to identify a species by its developing leaves, long before the flowers are out, can be challenging, but I would heartily recommend it. If the walk is one you take regularly, you can keep an eye on the species over subsequent months and, with a bit of luck, the answer will emerge along with the flower.

In early January, even though a grey pall can drape itself over every day, deep down in the soil those first movements of new life are stirring. For most, it is a time of dormancy or suspension, lying low, waiting for the earth to warm up. However, there are some brave souls in the plant world that manage to remain above ground all year round. Even during bone-chilling days of horizontal rain and biting winds, they do their utmost to show us their flowers.

Winter flowers tend to be small – and for good reason. By presenting a smaller profile to the elements there is less of them to be blown about or shrivelled up by the cold. A typical example is **Shepherd's-purse**, that spindly annual that seems to grow everywhere – borders of supermarket car parks, cracks in footpaths and unweeded suburban gardens. It manages in very poor soil, but tends to grow larger where the earth is more fertile. It has clusters of tiny white-petalled flowers and produces the little flat, heart-shaped seedpods for which it is named.

shepherd's-purse

There is one species whose flowers will always illuminate a winter's day, even on snow-covered hillsides. Known to some as Furze, to others as Whin, I know it as **Gorse**. It is the shrub of farmland, heaths and hedgerows. It is a mass of spines – in reality leaves that have evolved into rigid, furrowed thorns – and it bears crowded, golden spikes of coconut-smelling flowers. Although I once fell off my bike into the prickliest Gorse bush in County Wicklow, I lived to tell the tale. Its own ability to survive is undisputed. Its branches have a high concentration of oil, which helps to ignite it and it is frequently subject to being burned, even during the prohibited period (from 1 March to 31 August). Regrettably, with this burning, valuable habitat can be lost for other species of wildlife – literally in a flash.

Gorse's worth is vastly underrated. It offers protection to nesting birds, such as Wrens, Linnets, Stonechats and Blackbirds, giving them a safe haven,

Gorse

Daisy – from Old English 'dæges-eage' meaning day's eye

deep within its impenetrable vegetation, also providing habitat for small mammals and amphibians. Gorse helps to enrich the earth in which it grows. It belongs to the Peaflower family, as do beans, peas, soybeans, lentils, and peanuts – plants which help to keep us fed. Through small nodules in their deep roots, all the members of this family trap and collect nitrogen from the air, in turn passing this precious commodity into the earth.

How could we ever consider January's flowering plants without including the **Daisy**? Our little *Nóinín* is often seen during winter even though its principal flowering time is March to October. The Daisy is probably the one flower everybody knows. I cannot imagine there is a child who hasn't drawn it at some stage or made daisy chains or plucked its petals, chanting 'He loves me, he loves me not' until each petal has been removed. Perhaps it is so common that it goes unnoticed by most except for those who want a perfect, unblemished, manicured lawn. Daisies grow so tightly to the soil that they defy the best efforts of lawnmowers.

Their blades can never get low enough to chop the flower heads off. Chemical companies part gardeners from large amounts of money in an effort to remove these plants. Gardening tools such as one called the 'daisy grubber' have been created with the specific removal of Daisies in mind. I have a lawn, but I prefer a peaceful coexistence with nature. I treasure whatever arrives unbidden, tending to leave wild patches where nature has scattered some of her bounty.

As a child, I combed all sorts of places for **Groundsel** – our budgerigars loved it – so I got to recognise and appreciate its unremarkable features very early. It is possibly one of the most under-recorded of our native species. It is ubiquitous, in abundance almost everywhere – on wall tops, rubbish tips, gravel paths and gardens – all year round. But were the likes of Vincent van Gogh or Claude Monet ever tempted to paint its image? What illustrious writer ever tried to depict it in prose or poetry? It was used traditionally in herbal medicine to make poultices, its strange name coming from the Old English '*gundeswilge*', with '*gund*' meaning pus and '*swelgan*' meaning to swallow. Yuk. The name of its genus (Genus being the category in classification between Family and Species) is *Senecio* which comes from the Latin '*senex*' or old man – because Groundsel bears a pappus or seedhead of white hair.

Groundsel

Shepherd's-purse | *Capsella bursa-pastoris* | Lus an spáráin

Gorse | *Ulex europaeus* | Aiteann gallda

Daisy | *Bellis perennis* | Nóinín

Groundsel | *Senecio vulgaris* | Grúnlas

Common Chickweed

When I was a child, our neighbours fed **Common Chickweed** to their pet chinchilla rabbits. My father told me that at one time it was sold in markets, being considered a nutritious vegetable that tasted like spinach.

This is another species that flowers all year and, as it was also on our budgies' menu, I know it from way back. It is quite easy to identify. If you look closely at the stems, you can see a little line of soft hairs running along them – this clinches your identification. Look for its bright green leaves and its tiny, white star-like flowers around the bottom of trees in public parks, on streets, in abandoned flowerpots and in gardens. It even grows in tiny cracks in pavements and old walls.

The mention of our budgies ignites a spark that begins to flicker its way through some internal magic-lantern-like images from my childhood. The first picture shows two parents and their three young daughters, Janet, Zoë and Drusilla, packing a Commer station wagon. As the holiday paraphernalia is squeezed into the back of the car, space has to be left for a strange pair of holidaymakers – Bill and Coo. Our budgies came along with us every year, squawking and chattering all the way, scattering birdseed everywhere. They never seemed to object to their trip and they were, after all, part of the family.

My inner slide show continues, showing our first excited arrival in the early 1950s at what was to be home for the next two weeks. Somewhat unimaginatively called 'The Boat-house', it was a converted two-storey building beside a stone jetty in Derrynane, County Kerry. The lower storey had previously housed a few boats but now contained a kitchen and a small sitting room. Above, up a wooden ladder-type stairs, were two bedrooms. Far from the modern holiday homes of Celtic Tiger days, this was a functional dwelling. There was a little porch where our wellies and rain macs hung, often slowly dripping puddles across the concrete floor. The loo was a modest outdoor building, complete with the necessary apparatus. We got our water from a well a few hundred yards up the road, towards the nearby village of Caherdaniel. After we had our first supper, we climbed the stairs. It didn't take us long to fall asleep.

The next morning – it must have been five or six o'clock – we were woken by sunlight streaming in through the thin cotton curtains, illuminating the room with an intense radiance. In an unspoken agreement, we dressed ourselves and 'snuck' down the stairs. There wasn't a cheep out of Bill or Coo. They slept on in their cage, under the cover of a large woollen blanket. Lifting the latch of the wooden porch door, we let ourselves out.

The cool morning air raised little goosebumps on our arms, but the delight in our surroundings immunised us from any feeling other than pure bliss. The dwelling was right on the beach and we felt such a sense of freedom, running and skipping towards the low dunes where the Marram grasses swayed.

The sandy slopes behind the beach rose from a narrow fringe of barnacle-covered rocks, some of them jutting into the flat sand like long pointed fingers of stone. We ran across the flat expanse feeling the cool,

Left: L–r: Sisters Janet, Drusilla and Zoë in Derrynane
Centre: The author, aged nine
Right: The Boat-house in Derrynane

Derrynane Harbour with Deenish and Scariff as painted by Zoë

slightly soft sand beneath our bare feet – occasionally avoiding the cutting edges of empty razor shells. Suddenly we all stopped short, spreading our arms wide, rising onto our toes. We had run around a small sandy bank and come to a point where a sloping prong of rock was exposed. The constant action of the tide had gouged out a very large pool at its tip. To our eyes it was almost bottomless – probably being deeper than we were tall – and we sensed each other's fear with a chill of excitement.

The pool was crystal clear, becoming a darker blue towards the centre. Sea anemones waved their tentacles, like red and purple fingers, swaying with the moving swell of the water. A few little green crabs sidled across the sloping rocks where we could also see several Sea urchins. The far side of the pool bore Limpets of differing sizes and the telltale rings of earlier creatures. We were absolutely fascinated and it was tempting to stay there, enthralled, slightly scared but also captivated by the submarine landscape. But we realised we should get back before our absence was noticed. Somewhat reluctantly we turned for home and, as quietly as possible, we tiptoed up into our bedroom and slipped back into our beds.

We must have drifted back to sleep, probably dreaming of the blue pool across the beach. In some ways it seemed like it had only been an exciting dream but I can still feel the way the hairs on the back of my neck rose that day – and it wasn't just the sea breeze.

Common Chickweed | *Stellaria media* | Fliodh

Winter
Heliotrope

IT HAS A CERTAIN, quite distinctive, scent; some say vanilla, I'd say liquorice. **Winter Heliotrope** always conjures up memories of the time when I used to cycle from our house in Dundrum to Clonskeagh.

I had some cousins living there and during weekends and school holidays we knew how to enjoy ourselves. We would invariably take off to a nearby piece of woodland that bordered the River Dodder. Either side of the paths lay great carpets of these plants, crowding close to each other, like green scales, with spikes of pale pink flowers blooming throughout our Christmas holidays. We basked in the utter freedom of being completely unsupervised.

Winter Heliotrope beside the DART line between Glenageary and Dalkey

It was great, genuine, innocent fun, getting up to all sorts of divilment and no harm ever came from it.

Winter Heliotrope was introduced in the early nineteenth century by beekeepers who planted it near their hives to provide nectar for any early emerging bees. But just take a look at how it has galloped out into the wild since. Its pale kidney-shaped leaves clothe borders of motorways, railway embankments and sandy cliffs, smothering most of the other vegetation; at present Winter Heliotrope's status in the register of invasive species is 'medium impact'. This plant's only saving grace is its heavenly smell, which can be detected from quite a bit away.

Our wildflowers – and most of the biodiversity around us – are undoubtedly imperilled by our very existence and how we treat our planet. The decline in numbers of bees, butterflies, birds and plants is unquestionable and it is human activity that is responsible. There are many reasons why our native plants are declining, but a major threat comes from the spread of invasive aliens. Most of these species have been introduced into Ireland, quite innocently, by garden lovers and the industry that supports them. Not all introductions forget their manners and run wild, but a few do, and that is enough to cause problems, some of them major (see page 146) The habitats which suffer the most are freshwater river systems and ponds, woodlands, heaths and coastal regions.

Winter Heliotrope | *Petasites fragrans* | Plúr na gréine

Most wildflower guides refer to the 'flowering period' of different species; this is only ever an approximation. It really means the time when you are most likely to see them in blossom. Don't feel that you won't find them outside those months – some may be early bloomers, others late stragglers. There is always quite a difference between the first flowering in the north compared to that of the south of the country. If you come across a species, earlier or later than the time indicated in a book, it is not always a reason to feel you've made a mistake in your identification. If it's way off the mark, it is, perhaps, time to research a little deeper or seek the help of someone who knows more about the subject. Whatever the reason, it is a fact that these 'official flowering periods' are only rough steers.

So what is happening in the soil in January? Well, last year's annuals will have scattered their seeds and – except for those that fall by the wayside or have been devoured by the fowls of the air – they will start the process of germination when the warmth of the sun filters through to them. Biennials, beginning their first season, will be preparing to produce and display their leaves during the coming year. At some stage in year two, they will produce flowers. Perennials that died back in autumn will have stored, within their root system, the blueprint for their metamorphosis into flowering plants once again. And *we* think we're the clever ones!

In the months of winter, creeping underground roots such as the rhizomes of **Sea Bindweed** or **Water-lilies**, lie dormant until a certain

Sea
Bindweed

white
water-lilies

combination of light and heat triggers the formation of their new shoots. This form of vegetative reproduction can be observed in many of our perennials, but there is also a great number of species that store their food in simple bulbs during the dormancy period. Anybody who has ever planted Daffodil or Crocus bulbs correctly will know that the roots are located on the underside of the bulb with the growing point emerging from the top. So it is with our **Bluebells**, **Orchids** and many other monocotyledons. (Flowering plants are divided into two groups: Monocotyledons and Dicotyledons. Monocots are the smaller group and include plants with long, narrow, parallel-veined leaves – think of grasses

Bluebells at Tintern Abbey, County Wexford

and cultivated bulbs. Dicots have leaves that are branched and whose veins are reticulate or network-like – think of Ivy and Nettles.) Once the bulb has stopped flowering, the leaves go on to draw energy from the sun and soil, laying down the necessary nutrients for the following year's blooms.

Sea Bindweed | *Calystegia soldanella* | Plúr an phrionsa

White Water-lily | *Nymphaea alba* | Bacán bán

Bluebell | *Hyacinthoides non-scripta* | Coinnle corra

Common
Butterwort

WHILE LATE JANUARY might not be the time to find wildflowers in any numbers, it is always a useful time to scout out habitats which may have high yields in the months to come.

Some time in the early 1980s, I decided I wanted to learn more about two particular plants. Both tend to grow on nutrient-poor soils, such as bogs and mountains. Insectivorous species, they were **Common Butterwort** and **Round-leaved Sundew** and I particularly wanted to see a feature which was common to both of them, a *hibernaculum*. I had only read about it and wondered if there was the slightest chance of finding one for myself. In botany, a *hibernaculum* is a winter-resting bud or protective case that houses the organism of aquatic and terrestrial plants, such as Bladderworts, Sundews and Butterworts. The buds sink deep into the bottom of pools or wet ground and survive the winter there. They grow larger as spring approaches when they rise to the surface, allowing the species to regenerate. In my innocence, I thought I would know one when I saw it. Wrong again.

Some insectivorous plant species have evolved a way to sustain themselves in nutrient-poor soils by trapping small insects on their sticky leaves. With the help of certain enzymes, they digest the poor little bugs almost totally. In the case of Common Butterwort, the leaves spread out from the flower's stems, standing out in a star-shaped rosette. Pale green, their edges curl inwards slightly, bringing even more sticky glands in contact with their helpless victims. The purple, violet-like flower is held solitarily, at the top of a slender stem, high enough to keep any potentially useful pollinator well clear of the deathtrap below. In the case of the Round-leaved Sundew – our most common Sundew – the circular leaves are reddish, on long stalks that also fan out in a rosette. Each leaf has numerous hairs, each hair with a sticky little drop at its tip. In the same way as with Butterwort, when an insect lands on the leaf, it quickly gets trapped by the leaf rolling over and – literally – sucking the life out of it. The leaves are the most recognisable part of this species although it has little white flowers held aloft, in a small cluster, well away from the leaves. But I didn't expect to see either Sundew or Butterwort leaves on that cold winter day; it was way too early. It was the *hibernaculum* I was after.

Round-leaved Sundew

It was a cold, crisp morning. There were four of us – my husband, Pete, our friends Tony and Anne, and myself – and we drove into the Wicklow Mountains, parking beside Boleyhorrigan Bridge. This is where the R759 (Roundwood–Sallygap road) crosses a mountain stream, which at the time was in full spate as it tumbled down into Lough Tay. Our objective was Fancy Mountain also known as Luggala. Fancy Mountain (*Fuinnse*, meaning Rowan tree) lies within the Guinness estate and rises to a majestic 595 metres. Its situation, directly overlooking Lough Tay, is surely one of the most dramatic and spectacular sights in the Wicklow Mountains.

Fancy Mountain
with Lough Tay
in the foreground

We were taking the easy route, preferring to leave for some other day the more difficult eastern ascent. This would have taken us up a rock-strewn gully that rises steeply from the lakeshore to the craggy summit. Instead, our course took us across the valley floor, by way of a couple of streams that feed Lough Tay, and then gently up the northern flank of the mountain. The habitat seemed perfect for my two species.

Striking out briskly, the low, anaemic January sun barely warming us, we mullocked across the heathy turf, boots sinking at times in the squelchy ground. We crossed the lake's main contributing river by stepping stones and began to gain height. After an hour or so we were close to the summit and hunger began to get the better of us. Grub was swiftly eaten and flasks of hot tea were emptied.

The view was absolutely breathtaking – Djouce and War Hill on the opposite side of the valley were two mountains we'd been up earlier that winter. They looked so different from this angle. The lake below us was deep, inky-black and sinister in the shadow of the mountain. Overhead a Raven croaked its unmistakeable *kraark*.

It was getting colder so we decided not to prolong the pit stop. It would only take twenty minutes or so to reach the summit, to get the full 360-degree view of these hills. I was studying the vegetation, wondering what secrets lay hidden beneath the heathy, sometimes mossy ground. Then, quite suddenly, my right foot found a bit of uneven ground and wobbled. I heard a snap and felt a sharp pain in my ankle. The foot refused to bear my weight. I flopped to the ground and, pulling up my trouser leg, I could see that the ankle was already swelling. Anne emptied a bottle of cold water over her neck scarf and wrapped it around my ankle in an effort to reduce the swelling. Oh, was it painful! And worse, I had put an end to our lovely little expedition.

There was nothing to do but to get back to the car, as quickly as possible. Already very cold, the weather could easily change for the worse. Anne was given the task of carrying my rucksack as well as her own – fortunately we had eaten all the food so at least the bags were a little lighter. I was ordered to stand on my good leg, and Pete and Tony got either side of me, while I wrapped an arm around each of their necks. Progress was slow with three of us trying to proceed on five legs instead of six and Anne bringing up the rear, laden down fore and aft with backpacks.

My companions were great, helping me across the boggy turf, stopping every now and again to catch breath. We couldn't manage the stepping stones this time – it was too awkward – so we waded through the icy water. It was freezing but the numbing effect lent temporary relief to my ankle. We eventually reached the car and I know it was my three pals and a large rush of adrenaline that kept me going that afternoon.

Loughlinstown Hospital did their best for me. A large, white boot – heavy as a lump of concrete – was attached to my right leg, I was issued with crutches and told to come back in a fortnight. Maybe the adrenaline was still working because I was more than happy to quench my thirst on the way home, visiting our usual watering hole where I left a trail of damp plaster marks on the landlord's polished linoleum.

It was only the next morning, when I woke up and realised that the concrete boot was still there, that I felt my spirits drooping very, very low. I had spoiled everyone's trip up Fancy Mountain. I never tried it again and still haven't seen a *hibernaculum*.

Common Butterwort | *Pinguicula vulgaris* | **Bodán meascáin**
Round-leaved Sundew | *Drosera rotundifolia* | **Drúchtín móna**

ivy-leaved
Toadflax

Feabhra

February

After the Latin term 'februum',
meaning purification · Third month
of the meteorological winter in Ireland
and shortest month of the year

T HE FIRST DAY OF FEBRUARY, *Lá Fhéile Bríde*, is traditionally observed in Ireland as the feast day of St Brigid. 'February fill-dyke' was what my English grandmother called this month of wet ditches, soggy fields and sometimes melting snow. It is a time of cold, damp, gloomy weather and although there is the possibility of the occasional clear bright day, it does not seem to happen too often.

February is also my birthday month and in 1950 our next-door neighbour, Betty Connell, gave me one of the best birthday presents ever. It was a copy of *Birds, Trees and Flowers* published in 1947. Among the contributors were Brian Vesey-Fitzgerald, Sir William Beach Thomas and Eleanor Vachell, who wrote chapters entitled 'Characteristics of Birds', 'The Living Tree' and 'Wayside Flowers' respectively.

How I devoured that book! I pored over it endlessly until I knew all there was to know about everything – or so I thought. Only a few colour illustrations graced its pages; they were excellent but the photographs were in black and white. It was left to the inner eye to imagine how a grey Cowslip might actually look in its livery of bright yellow, or how the off-white berries of Cuckoo-pint might turn out to be scarlet.

A year later, my godmother and her husband gave me *The Observer's Book of British Wild Flowers*, which provided information about 200 British species. Some of these plants didn't grow in Ireland but there were plenty that did. The book was extremely informative and it fitted in my pocket, so I could bring it with me on early nature walks.

I spent a few more years observing nature, and wildflowers in particular, before I was lucky enough to obtain a book that dealt exclusively with species to be found on this island. This was *An Irish Flora*, written by David Allardice Webb who, for several decades, was Ireland's leading botanist. First published in 1943 by Dundalgan Press Limited (which has been publishing books for over 150 years), *An Irish Flora* ran to seven editions and was recently reissued as *Webb's An Irish Flora* in homage to this great Irish botanist. David Webb (1912–1994) was highly regarded, not only in Irish botanical circles but internationally.

A pocket-sized hardback, *An Irish Flora* contained instructions for 'keying out' plant species. 'Keying out' is a method of identification that is basically a type of elimination contest where various features of a plant are scrutinised in depth. Depending on the result of this analysis, an aspiring botanist can continue through many stages of close examination, ultimately arriving at an identification. Not for a total beginner, this method takes some time to learn, but

Webb's 'An Irish Flora' and Colgan's 'Flora of the County Dublin'

it is worth the effort. In his book, Webb also encouraged amateurs to participate in field trips – he reckoned they were the best way to learn. He described the various habitats in Ireland and the regions where rare plants might be found. He also stressed the importance of areas without rarities but where other not-so-common species could possibly occur. David Webb was responsible for many other publications and also held the chair in Botany at Trinity College Dublin for a number of years.

In 2008, I was lucky enough to obtain a copy of a book published in 1904, entitled *Flora of the County Dublin* by Nathaniel Colgan. A self-taught naturalist, Colgan's main fields of interest were botany and molluscs. His *Flora* is extremely interesting and, as a Dubliner, I can see for myself that although a large number of wildflowers were present in the county up to 1904, many of them are now absent. For example, Colgan wrote of **Yellow Horned-poppy** (see page vi) being recorded 'between Sandymount and Merrion and at Killiney Bay … [in] 1857'. A distinctive species with fleshy, blue-green leaves, large, four-petalled yellow flowers and curved, horn-like seedpods, it is no longer found in any of these locations. It is now mainly confined to a relatively small number of sites on the east and south coasts.

My treasured copy of Colgan's book came with a name and date handwritten inside the front cover. I was curious as to who had previously owned it. The inscription read 'Oleg Polunin 1950'. I subsequently learned that Oleg Vladimirovitch Polunin (1914–85) was an English botanist who wrote many authoritative guides to the flora of Europe and the Himalaya. I was so pleased to learn that he had also spent some time recording flowering plants and ferns on Sherkin and other County Cork islands in Roaringwater Bay during the 1940s, around the time when I was learning to walk and talk. It gives me great pleasure to hold this book in my hands, both for the amazing data it contains about my home county, but also for the fact that before it came into my possession it was in the hands of such an illustrious botanist.

Yellow Horned-poppy | *Glaucium flavum* | Caillichín na trá

A LARGE PART of my formative years was spent attending a convent school in Dublin. To the rear of a rickety old bicycle shed that housed our precious Raleighs and Rudges was an area where a few of us used to sneak, and where we thought we were safe from the nuns' eyes. A vegetable garden lay before us: old moss-covered apple trees lining the pathways around rectangular patches of cabbages and onions. Behind us, as we sat on a low granite wall, was the chapel.

What were we doing there? Learning to smoke, of course! How we thought we would get away with it I don't know and, of course, we eventually got into trouble, but it was all part of growing up. We would sit there, trying to conquer the dizziness that accompanied our first, tentative 'drags' on shared Woodbines, wafting away the telltale smoke, along with our guilt perhaps – or was it our innocence? We often spent our lunch hours there, sitting in our gymslips, giggling, bums frozen, thoughts running in so many directions – 'what if we're caught, what would our parents say?' But there was another part of my mind that, even then, had begun to wander off in a different direction. I was taking in something else as well as nicotine and in retrospect it was a lot healthier.

My radar had detected an abundance of small plants growing on those walls. They were **Ivy-leaved Toadflax**, a species introduced into Ireland

Less common white version of Ivy-leaved Toadflax

from the Mediterranean region about 400 years ago. It is a trailing plant with lilac-coloured flowers whose shape resembles miniature Snapdragons. It has two upper petals and a lovely, generous, three-lobed lower lip with two splotches of yellow at the opening into the 'dragon's' mouth. It grows mainly on limestone or mortared walls, and it has an ingenious mechanism for ensuring next year's generation. The flowers turn their heads up to the sun until they have been fertilised, then they twist around towards the wall they are growing on, pushing the seeds into any little niche or crevice in order for them to develop.

They also have long roots, which help them to hang on, guaranteeing the survival of their species. Found at almost any time of the year, they are particularly fresh and bright from February to November. When I was in Cork, a couple of years ago, I found a white-flowered version growing on the walls bordering the River Lee. It looked rather anaemic and I must say that I prefer the more common lilac-coloured form (see page 21).

Now, from my lofty, non-smoker's perch, when I look at that little flower growing on my own garden wall, it always takes me back to that place in my youth and our happy-go-lucky, gymslipped giggles.

Ivy-leaved Toadflax | *Cymbalaria muralis* | **Buaflíon balla**

PLEASURES OFTEN come in twos. In the case of County Wicklow's Vartry Reservoir, there are twin treats which Pete and I like to award ourselves early each year. One is always easy enough to spot, but the other is definitely down to Lady Luck.

Always a favourite walk, if good fortune shines upon us during winter, we might just time it right and find that the Whooper Swans have arrived for their annual visit. From October to April they desert their breeding grounds in Iceland and can be seen – and heard – on some of our lakes, estuaries and sheltered coastal areas where they overwinter. Often foraging inland, they fly some distances from their roosts to graze on suitable pasture and stubble, with potatoes, acorns and spilt grain being very much part of their diet. They make loud, resonant, trumpeting calls in flight and are extremely sociable birds, congregating in big flocks. The largest number of Whooper Swans we have seen at this location is thirteen and believe me when I tell you that that small band of remarkable creatures was greeted with whoops of delight.

Bordering the path which runs along the reservoir are drainage ditches where our second treat grows. Sometimes as early as January, the flowers of **Lesser Celandine** begin to decorate the sides of these channels, glowing like shiny golden suns on their bed of glossy, heart-shaped leaves, each decorated with an intricate pattern of deep veins and dark markings. The petals gleam as if they were polished and if you turn them over, the reverse side is an unexpected bronze. These are definitely our heralds of spring.

Lesser Celandine

Whooper Swans on the Vartry Reservoir in County Wicklow

When I was writing this piece, I realised I didn't have any good photographs of Whooper Swans — I never had a long lens with me when they were around — what images I had were enough for identification but not as good as I wanted them to be. It was February so I decided to go out specially to find them, knowing that it could end up as a wild-goose chase. I packed a long lens this time, and set off for the reservoir; however, there was no sign of the birds. Kind people at BirdWatch Ireland suggested Kilcoole, a large wetland complex on the coast of County Wicklow, where they had been spotted a few days earlier. We arrived at Kilcoole quite early, along with about 200 walkers, most of whom, it seemed, had at least two dogs. After walking for some time we spotted a group of six of the swans on a small patch of ground jutting into the lagoon. The wind was biting, absolutely bone-numbing and the creatures, very wisely, had their heads tucked under their wings. I put the camera on the tripod, Pete did the same with his scope and we waited for the birds to lift their heads … and we waited. Dogs were coming up to us, being inquisitive. One was lifting his leg against my camera bag when I caught sight of him. His owners weren't at all impressed with my roar. The dogs kept on coming. It wasn't very helpful and I had a little rant to myself about dog owners and their obligations to society. Pete had heard it all before.

The birds remained as immobile as statues, their heads still out of sight. Then, for just a nano-second, one lifted its head and I could see the defining beak shape. In the Whooper Swan, the bill is yellow and black, with the yellow projecting below its nostril. Our resident Mute Swan's bill is orange-red and it has a prominent knob on its forehead. Then, before I could press the shutter release, the head went back under the wing, swiftly. Who could blame it, but it wasn't going to make a good enough photograph.

Brent Goose

Two young Otters

And that's when I got the surprise of my life. As I peered through my lens, entering from right and running to the left were, not one, but two young otters. My finger pressed the shutter release repeatedly while I shouted to Pete like a woman possessed. I was trying to tell him where they were, while following them through the camera lens, as they scampered southwards. They frolicked, they jumped, they teased and played with one another until they got to the water's edge where they continued their leaping and cavorting straight on into the water. Every now and again a tail would emerge, pointing skywards. Small waves betrayed where they were swimming, just breaking the surface only to dive back down. We watched until we could see them no more. What a thrill! Neither of us had ever seen two otters together before. It more than made up for the lack of a Whooper Swan image. That would have to come another day.

We returned the following week, but there were no Whoopers and we were becoming no-hopers. Just as we were about to turn and go home, we heard a strange sound. At first it seemed like some children were chattering to each other, close by, all at the same time. Then we realised it was coming from overhead. A flock of Brent Geese flew over our heads in a perfect skein, slowly circling around and settling down on the surface of the lough. They were such smartly turned-out birds, with black heads, dark-brown wings and pale underparts. On the side of each neck was a little mark like a splash of white paint. They settled themselves in the lough and slowly paddled towards us. The shutter release was put to good use. It was pure magic.

Lesser Celandine | *Ficaria verna* | **Grán arcáin**

EVERY YEAR, when I get the first distinct, celery-like whiff of **Alexanders**, I am transported to the place I knew as paradise, once upon a time.

Alexanders is a tall, shiny-leaved plant that lines many roadsides in early spring. It has been extremely successful at making itself at home in Ireland. Now completely naturalised, it was introduced into these islands by the Romans who used it in their cooking in the way we use celery, often blanching it or eating it raw in salads.

Alexanders on North Bull Island, Dublin

o Foxglove

As it tolerates salt well, it is found more widely in coastal regions. I have noticed recently how it has freshly colonised areas where I never saw it in the past so it is obviously very clever at spreading. A biennial, it produces umbels of creamy white flowers that in turn become black seeds once used as a flavouring, somewhat like black pepper.

My sisters and I had two pals who lived next-door-but-one. Our houses had long, narrow gardens where most of our vegetables were grown and hens were kept. At the far end of the garden, beyond the plum and greengage trees, Dad had built a swing where we could soar like birds, high above the privet hedge. But best of all, through an old wooden gate and beyond, lay Heaven, a place which, with striking originality, we called 'the Back Lane'. Behind a grassy bank and making our Heaven into an utter utopia, was a little river. This, I have subsequently learnt, was the River Slang (*Abhainn na Stéille*) which, from its origins in Three Rock Mountain, flows through Dundrum and becomes a tributary of the River Dodder at Milltown, eventually becoming part of the Liffey.

We spent blissful hours in that river, fishing for tiddlers and whatever else might swim our way. During the school holidays, from dawn to dusk we poked around, nudging mossy rocks to make dams, floating little wooden boats, the hems of our summer frocks tucked into the legs of our knickers. We scooped up tiny fish – 'pinkeens' – with fishing rods made from bamboo. Bent over our tasks, we applied an enthusiasm and focus not given to any of our scholastic endeavours. We only reappeared from this blissful activity when we got called in for refuelling. Afterwards, the milk moustache wiped off with the back of our hands, the liquid still gurgling in our tummies, we would run back down to continue whatever task we had embarked on earlier. Perhaps it was picking **Foxgloves** to wear on our fingers or sticking

Fuchsia

long, pointed magenta **Fuchsia** sepals on our fingernails, pretending to be princesses at the very least. Our imaginations were unlimited.

Each summer, our immediate neighbours, the Murphys, had one of their cousins from 'down the country' to stay with them for a few weeks. This was Paddy who was the same age as me. He showed me how to whittle sticks with a penknife, construct a bow and arrow, and make the noise of a howling fox by blowing through a blade of grass, sandwiched between my thumbs. But what I remember best, and what I am reminded of by the aroma of Alexanders, is the year we built our 'house'.

In springtime, fresh Alexanders plants are supple and strong, glossy and green, but by the time of our summer holidays the freshness of spring was long past. They were now brittle and faded to a shade of dry ochre. Paddy and I methodically cut down Alexander stems, stripped them of their wilted, yellowed leaves and, using the remaining stalks, we wove and knitted together a small cupboard-sized house. In reality it was just big enough for the two of us but our make-believe was enough to make it a mansion. We spent hours in this dreamland, telling each other stories and secrets, never to be revealed on pain of death. Each night our house would fall down and each day we would rebuild it. It was an occupation of which we never tired. We must have devastated the Alexanders crop that year.

I suppose we had to grow out of our back lane and our Alexanders paradise, but when I get that unique scent each spring it connects me to a little piece of my childhood. Incidentally, I recently came across this entry on Wikipedia: 'The Slang was a small stream in a grassy glen behind Dundrum's main street, near the old Dundrum Castle, and children used to play there until late in the 1960s, from when it was confined more and more by modern developments.'

Alexanders | *Smyrnium olusatrum* | Lusrán grándubh

Foxglove | *Digitalis purpurea* | Lus mór

Fuchsia | *Fuchsia magellanica* | Fiúise or Deora Dé

Woodland at Harristown, County Wexford

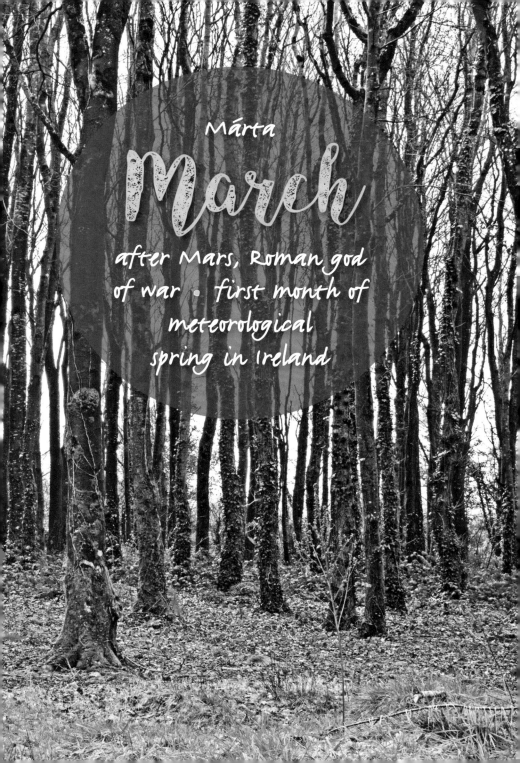

Márta

March

after Mars, Roman god
of war • first month of
meteorological
spring in Ireland

O RIGINALLY THE ROMAN CALENDAR only had ten months. March was the first month of the year, April the second month and so on, all the way to December, the tenth month. The Julian calendar was introduced in 46 BC, based on the movements of the moon, and January was decreed to be the first month, but this was not widely accepted and was reversed by the Council of Tours in 567 AD. However, in the sixteenth century the Gregorian calendar confirmed January as the first month of the year and it gradually became widely accepted over the next two centuries, confirming March as the third month.

This is the month when a few of our spring flowers appear, poking their heads above ground, braving the March winds, fighting the last vestiges of winter's chill. 'In like a lion, out like a lamb' went the old adage describing this unpredictable month. 'March winds and April showers bring forth May's flowers' was another saying I heard as a child and, as with a large amount of folklore, there is frequently an element of truth attached.

The soil begins to warm by a couple of degrees in March and the hours of daylight will be on the increase until mid-June. These two factors signal the beginnings of growth for many of our plant species. In the last week of March, daylight saving time means we put our clocks forward by an hour and this often coincides with the beginning of brighter days. I have often heard the old country maxim that claims each day stretches by 'a hen's step' until summer arrives.

Even though the clocks have gone forward, it can still be unrelentingly cold and rainy in March. However, in my morning shower I not only feel water flowing over me but enthusiasm and pure, untarnished optimism.

Impatient for spring to begin and the wildflowers to start showing their heads, I have taken to doing a bit of birdwatching in March, spending many chilly hours trying to focus my eyes and attention on the small, faraway details that help to identify our avian friends. I have passed a lot of time on the shores of Bannow Bay in County Wexford. On one particular day in March, while the tide was falling, I was at the wide, flat, muddy estuary where two rivers, the Corock and the Owenduff, become one

Bannow Bay, County Wexford

Shelduck

watercourse, a little west of Wellingtonbridge. I had hoped to get a good look at, and perhaps a photograph of, a Shelduck, a most handsome duck I had spotted a few days earlier while driving by – me, not the duck. This is a creature that can be either a resident or a migrant to Ireland. During the winter months, our native population is increased by visitors from Scandinavia and the Baltics. It is a colourful, medium-sized bird with plumage of chestnut, black and white. It has a distinctive red bill, the male having a prominent knob at the base. It feeds on small aquatic snails and crabs in sheltered estuaries and tidal areas such as mudflats, and Bannow Bay is its textbook habitat.

An hour or so earlier, I had been looking across the flat expanse of the bay, trying to focus my binoculars on the muddy stretch at the other side. A strip of shingle lay in front of the small channel of water that slowly flowed towards the sea. All of a sudden, as if a starting pistol had been fired, the shingle bank took to the air in one body. This was no shingle; this was an enormous flock of small waders who had been resting at the water's edge – possibly several hundred – but they had been startled. They soared – en masse – swaying and swinging in tight formation, veering and alternating their course as they headed away towards the sea. The light caught them each time they turned together, as if by a secret instruction, changing the colour of this amazing phenomenon from dark black to a pearly white through shades of silvery grey until they became a small pale cloud that grew smaller and smaller as they flew out to sea.

As I gathered up my scattered belongings to head for home, I noticed with delight a species of wildflower that I have always found most attractive and engaging. Lurking at the edge of the estuary was **Colt's-foot**, a small perennial that grows on waste ground, light sandy soil and beside rivers, usually first seen on south-facing banks. Think of a small child's drawing of the sun and you have Colt's-foot. With narrow yellow rays surrounding a darker yellow centre, the little flower head sits at the top of a downy, scale-covered stem that begins to emerge from the soil in February, long before the bright green, kidney-shaped leaves appear. Being one of quite a small

Colt's-foot

Great Northern Diver fishing

number of plants available to early-flying bees, Colt's-foot flowering is seen by many as beneficial, unless you are a gardener or park-keeper, who views the plant as a scourge.

Later that week, Pete and I took our binoculars over to Kilmore Quay, where the cold wind was rippling the surface of the water, creating 'cat's paws' – even inside the harbour. As we gazed towards the Saltee Islands, I spotted a seabird, diving and surfacing, every few minutes it seemed. Pete told me it was a Great Northern Diver, foraging for its survival. Overwintering in Ireland, far from its breeding grounds in Greenland or North America, this bird's diet consists of seafood mainly, Pete told me, and, as if to prove him right, it surfaced, carrying a large fish in its bill. My camera took that occasion to act up. However, later in the year I photographed a similar bird in its extremely handsome breeding plumage, also fishing for its dinner, off Black Head in County Clare.

Colt's-foot | *Tussilago farfara* | Sponc

Rue-leaved
saxifrage

I SUPPOSE I AM a bit odd, but often what I recall most about a place is the vegetation growing there. For instance, I visited the Coliseum in Rome a few years ago and what struck me most was the number of different species of wildflowers that grew all over it. Admittedly, the building was quite remarkable, but give me nature any day.

Some decades ago, we had a quartet of American cousins staying with us for a few weeks in late March. They naturally wanted to see as much of Ireland as they could during their visit and were particularly interested in

The Rock of Cashel

old castles and historical artefacts. It was this interest that prompted us to take them to see the Rock of Cashel in County Tipperary. The traditional seat of the kings of Munster prior to the Norman invasion, this is an extremely impressive collection of buildings, demonstrating Celtic art and medieval architecture. At the time of our visit, those three words 'health and safety' had not come into common parlance and if you wanted to do something silly, nobody was going to stop you. As a result, more of the buildings were accessible to the public than is the case now and so we found ourselves at a considerable height, gazing across the Munster landscape from an elevated part of the structure. However, my eye was drawn to a small plant that was growing on the very top of the wall we were leaning on. Until that moment I had never seen it, but I knew that it had to be **Rue-leaved Saxifrage.** Bearing a small white flower on red stems with fleshy, sticky, hairy green-red leaves in a rosette at the base of the plant, it could not be anything else. An indicator of medieval settlements, it is frequently found on old masonry, having a preference for sunny, alkaline conditions. My poring over books during the winter months had helped me to identify this little species and finding it unexpectedly, as I did, was such a bonus. I think our American cousins had already written me off as a bit eccentric; now it was confirmed.

Rue-leaved Saxifrage | *Saxifraga tridactylites* | **Móran balla**

Thale Cress on stony ground

APART FROM THE roaring noise and accompanying wind from a passing train, railway lines are relatively undisturbed places if you are a wildflower.

Many species have been spread through the country along railway tracks, seeds blowing around in the wake of the train. In much the same way, rivers tend to assist floating seeds to colonise riverbanks, and our motorways help salt-loving plants to migrate away from coastal regions, following a winter's salting of roads. I don't know if my find at Kilkenny railway station was blown to the Marble City or if, being classed as a native plant, its forebears had already been there for at least five centuries.

I was waiting for the train back to Dublin after visiting a friend in Kilkenny. As is often the case, I was early. There was a chilly wind blowing along the track as I walked up and down the platform, trying to keep warm.

White flowers and seedpods of Thale Cress

At one end, there was a ramp down to the level of the track and I peered into the area beyond it. It was being used as an unauthorised receptacle for cigarette ends, empty crisp bags and drink cans. Then I saw the straggliest, skinniest, spindliest, weediest little plant ever – its leaves were blotchy brown and dull green and on a long slender stem it bore a little cluster of small white flowers. Long, slightly curved seedpods stuck out from the stem below the flowers, like fish bones. I had never seen this one, nor did I remember it from the books, but it had to be the most unmemorable-looking flower I have ever seen.

I took several photographs and when I got home I identified it as **Thale Cress**, a most interesting species from a scientific point of view, its style belying its substance. It is now the plant of choice for scientists researching how plants work. Most of what is known about plant physiology, morphology and development has come from studying this little species. It has a very tiny genome (the genetic life-code of the species) and its main advantage is that because it is of little commercial value – which would not be the case with rice, for instance – researchers are free to exchange results without having to be concerned about patents. The plant is self-pollinating and, since it has not been genetically changed by plant breeding, anywhere it grows, it grows as a wild plant only. Its genes are its very own, not those achieved by cross-fertilisation or any artificial breeding. It grows extremely quickly, with a life cycle lasting about six weeks from germination to seed production, when it produces masses of seeds. This short generation cycle, together with its small size, makes it ideal for research purposes. One thousand of these plants would fit in the space where only twenty maize plants could squeeze. This has led some scientists to consider it possibly the most important plant in the world. And there it was, minding its own business and growing quietly among the litter of city commuters.

Thale Cress | *Arabidopsis thaliana* | Tailís

PETE'S FACE FELL, disgust etched all over it. He put his fork down and looked at his plate, his eyebrows making an inverted 'V'. 'I'm not really that hungry', he muttered, sorrowfully shaking his head.

He crossed the kitchen, opened the breadbin and, after a forage in the cupboard came back to the table with a couple of slices of bread and a pot of jam. I put a fork into my plate of steaming pasta, twisted it around and took some, passing it into my mouth in curious anticipation. It was inedible. I had hoped that mixing the homemade pesto into the cooked pasta would, somehow, lift it into another zone. But no, it was absolutely dreadful. I suppose it's all a matter of taste. There would seem to be hordes of people who love it … I never did like the idea of belonging to a horde, anyway.

Ramsons

I've been making pesto for quite a few years, using basil as the main flavouring ingredient. I'd read that Ramsons also makes a good pesto so I thought I'd give it a try. **Ramsons** is a very pretty native plant that carpets the woodland floor in early spring. Clusters of white, starlike flowers and broad, light-green leaves fill the space between deciduous trees in many parts of Ireland. One of two species commonly called Wild Garlic, it is known in some countries as 'Bear's Garlic', being a delicacy sought out by bears and wild boars. Perhaps bears and boars have different taste buds from mine.

Most of the recipes said 'pick a few handfuls', so I did. Feeling like Mother Earth, I washed them very carefully and blitzed them in the whizzer with some expensive virgin olive oil, to-die-for Parmesan cheese and toasted pine nuts. I tasted the resulting green goo … Not great, but perhaps the heat of the pasta would bring out a better flavour. It didn't.

If anything it was even worse, and the pasta and the goo became an expensive contribution to the compost heap. Suddenly Pete's bread and jam seemed like a good choice for lunch that day. The Ramsons in the little patch of woodland up the road are quite safe.

These days, foraging has become quite popular. Perhaps people want to get back to their roots on this planet by a connection with nature as their sustainer. In my childhood, I spent many holidays at my grandmother's house in the country. We hadn't heard of the word 'foraging', but we picked field mushrooms in early autumn mornings, large, wide, meaty umbrellas, which were sliced up and cooked with rashers of bacon and tasted incredibly good. We plucked blackberries from the hedgerows, gathered elderflowers, and picked sloes from the blackthorn bushes behind her house. She made jars and jars of jam, sparkling cordials and sloe gin – I was never allowed to taste the latter. Those were the days when the world wasn't quite as full as it is now and when there were far more places where wild plants could grow, unhindered.

I'm not against foraging but it can mean death to a plant – or even a human being – if not done correctly. The ethical guidelines for foraging say 'Always leave more than you take'. So, in theory, the first person could take 49 per cent, and the next person could take 49 per cent of what they found. In a short time there would be very little left. Most of the rules seem to be for the protection of those who are foraging, which, while important, doesn't say much for a caring attitude to the plants. I feel it's best done very sensitively, the sensitivity being directed to the plants. Nature should not be harmed by the consumer. If you have a garden, why not

Garlic bread

have one corner for wildlife, complete with nettles to be shared with butterflies, bees and other insects together with your soup-making needs? A few brambles, for jams and tarts also help our little pollinators.

To get back to my culinary efforts, I then picked some leaves from the other 'Wild Garlic' species, **Three-cornered Garlic,** which grows in a large spreading mass in our garden. Also known as Three-cornered Leek, it is so-named for its three-angled stems. Individually the flowers are very pretty, somewhat like a six-lobed white bluebell, with one green line running through each of the lobes. We have loads of it but I wasn't going to go down the pesto path again. This time, I used the leaves to make garlic bread. I washed them and chopped them finely, mixed them with butter and spread the mix between the almost-cut-through slices of French sticks. Fifteen minutes in a hot oven produced a tasty and tangy – and also edible – snack, far more successful than the pesto.

Apart from the flavour, there is another reason why it is better to use this species than Ramsons. Three-cornered Garlic is an introduced species and is quite a pest (oh!) as it tends to take over and crowd out native flora, especially in the sunny south-east. A bulbous perennial, it covers the ground very quickly, often aided by ants, which carry off its seeds. Having eaten part of the seed, they discard enough to help the species to spread – an example of good foraging behaviour on the part of the ants. So by foraging for Three-cornered Garlic, this time you are giving nature a helping hand.

Three-cornered Garlic | *Allium triquetrum* | Glaschrreamh

Ramsons | *Allium ursinum* | Creamh

Three-cornered garlic

No mention of March would be complete without a few words on the subject of **Lesser Trefoil**. Scientifically known as *Trifolium dubium*, Lesser Trefoil is the main contender for the species we call Shamrock, our national symbol. Legend has it that St Patrick used the Shamrock as a metaphor for the Christian Trinity and for many years there has been discussion and argument as to which species is the real Shamrock, with a few others of the Pea family in contention. Perhaps it is **White Clover,** which was recorded here as far back as 1727 and a plant the Irish botanist Caleb Threlkeld (1676–1728) wrote of as 'worn by the People in their Hats upon the Seventeenth day of March yearly'. Then again, it could be **Red Clover,** which was Linnaeus's favoured species for the title. Swedish-born Karl Linnaeus (1707–1778) was the botanist, physician and zoologist who was responsible for the modern binomial naming scheme for plants and animals. Almost two centuries earlier, English herbalist John Gerard (1545–1612) held the view that it was either the Red or the White Clover.

In order to try to resolve the question of which was the actual, authentic and valid species, the National Botanic Gardens in Dublin carried out a survey, not once but twice, in 1888 and 1983. All across Ireland, people were asked to send in plants they considered to be 'Shamrock'. The plants were grown on and when the flowers emerged a couple of months later, a count was taken. The surveys were almost a century apart, but there were only very small differences between them. About half of the specimens turned out to be Lesser Trefoil, with White Clover coming a close second. Down the list came Red Clover, **Black Medick,** and even **Wood-sorrel** was chosen by some who participated in the second survey. If any one of these species was unique to Ireland, there might have been a reason to think of it as our Shamrock. There is no clear winner. Our '*Seamair óg*', or young clover, will still be worn proudly on St Patrick's Day and will still be 'drowned'. Regardless of what species it is, the shamrock will always be our national emblem.

'shamrocks'

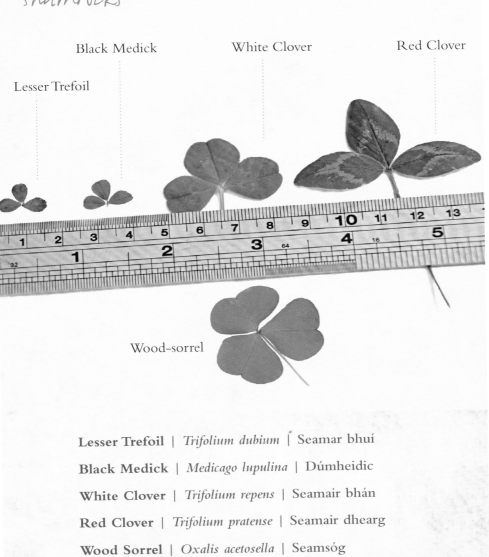

Lesser Trefoil

Black Medick

White Clover

Red Clover

Wood-sorrel

Lesser Trefoil | *Trifolium dubium* | Seamar bhuí

Black Medick | *Medicago lupulina* | Dúmheidic

White Clover | *Trifolium repens* | Seamair bhán

Red Clover | *Trifolium pratense* | Seamair dhearg

Wood Sorrel | *Oxalis acetosella* | Seamsóg

seen on the wing in march

An interest in wildflowers has resulted in my being exposed to other aspects of the environment. Birds, butterflies, insects of all sorts and an occasional mammal have crossed my path at one stage or another and added to my appreciation of nature.

As we get in sight of the kinder part of the year, I'd like to begin sharing with you just a little about our butterflies. Some have shorter flying periods than others, but most of them are around for a few of the warmer months. Like some half-remembered dreams, these ethereal wisps of aerial delight fly in and out of our days, enhancing our lives. Without them, and all of our pollinators, our future would be bleak.

Even in the early stages of spring, the **Small Tortoiseshell** was always the most common butterfly I knew as a child. Bracketing our butterfly flight season, it is typically the first species on the wing each year and the last to be seen in winter. Before the Painted Lady and Comma found their way to Ireland, this brightly coloured insect was known by all who noticed the natural world around them. On silky wings – a myriad of tiny, mosaic-like scales – it usually flies in gardens, searching for nectar in a wide variety of plants. Long after the sun's rays cease to warm their lives, these little creatures are often found overwintering in cupboards, behind heavy curtains and under poorly lit shelves. In common with the Red Admiral and the Peacock, their larval foodplant is **Common Nettle.** The term 'larval foodplant' means the plant the creatures lay their eggs on and upon which the larvae will depend for their nourishment. Please don't forget to leave a good patch of nettles in your garden on which they can breed and feed. The butterfly in my picture is seeking out nectar and, in so doing,

small Tortoiseshell

pollinating a recent arrival to our shores, **Narrow-leaved Ragwort.** This wildflower species is mainly found on rough waste ground close to seaports, and it is most likely that it first entered Ireland, undetected, among imported product about twenty years ago. With the typical yellow daisy flowers of the Ragwort genus, it is also known as South African Ragwort, where it is a native species.

Narrow-leaved Ragwort | *Senecio inaequidens*

Bridge at Inistioge, County Kilkenny

Aibreán

April

possibly from the Latin
'Aprilis', after 'aperire'
meaning 'to open' — when
so many flowers open
their buds • second
month of spring

A PRIL IS ONE OF THE MONTHS when Easter is celebrated, Primroses and Violets abound and newborn lambs gambol in the fields. Which of us is immune to the positive lift of this month as the evenings become brighter, stretching further with every day? My expectations of the months to come and what they may bring are boundless. But there is one element of spring I am loathe to let pass by, and that is from nature's bounty, in the form of an incredibly healthy dish.

From the **Common Nettle** comes an extremely tasty product which merits the title 'Super Food' – it is Nettle soup. Not only do nettles purify the blood but they are full of vitamins C and D. They also contain calcium and iron, along with many other welcome properties, so they are full of goodness. This soup is simple to make. However, you must ensure that the nettles are unpolluted and that you use long, strong gardening gloves to pluck them. Pick the leaves when they are young, preferably just taking the top four or five whorls. If they have started to flower, it is too late – they may contain a substance which could irritate your stomach. Pull the leaves from the stalks and wash them carefully and, if you follow this recipe, I am sure it will become a favourite spring lunchtime dish.

Nettles

Common Nettle | *Urtica dioica* | **Neantóg**

Nettle soup

Ingredients

1 tbsp of oil

1 onion chopped

1 leek – sliced

1 carrot – sliced

1 potato – sliced

1 litre of vegetable
or chicken stock

450g/1lb of nettles

Method

Heat the oil over a gentle heat.

Add the vegetables and cook for 15 minutes.

Add the stock and cook for another 10–15 minutes.

Add the nettle leaves and cook until they have
wilted.

Blend thoroughly, sieving if necessary to remove
any 'threads' from the nettles.

Reheat and ladle into soup bowls.

Float a small blob of whipped cream or crème
fraiche on top.

A few added nettle leaves give it a bit of style!

Enjoy.

WE HELD EACH other's gaze for what seemed like ten minutes, but I think, on reflection, it must have been very much less. It was, however, long enough for me to take in every detail of this image and store it for subsequent relish.

I was in Inistioge in County Kilkenny, a place worth visiting in any season. It was some years ago when I first explored this part of the world to see what it had to offer botanically. I came across a large, extremely wet area of ground, tucked under a line of beech trees that separated a lush, green meadow from the nearby road. As I ducked under the low branches to see what might lie at the back of this swampy ground, a lovely sight met my eyes. There stood a large group of **Summer Snowflake** – tall, elegant plants, with green-spotted, white, bell-shaped flowers, a bit like Snowdrops in high heels. I have read that the seeds of this plant are often spread by floating down rivers. Perhaps that's how they found themselves carried into the wetter regions of this meadow. The River Nore, which wends its way alongside it, often overflows in winter, leaving wet patches in its wake.

Summer Snowflake is one of those plants that look better when photographed from low down and the only way to do the job properly was to lie flat on the ground. It was very damp in that meadow, especially where the plants had chosen to grow. I was wearing wellies and had a large black bin bag with me, so I spread it out and prostrated myself. My elbows were braced, my two hands holding the camera steady. Just as I was about to press the shutter release, I became aware of some movement at the edge of my vision. I took the camera away from my eyes and turned my head slowly. It was a fox.

He stood still as a statue, absolutely motionless and our eyes met. A plan to try to photograph him came in and out of my mind with the speed of light. No, I would not even attempt to capture this beauty's image, I would just look and look and look. The tableau of the russet-coloured creature, his pointed muzzle with its outstanding black whiskers, his erect ears, white belly and long bushy tail are etched across my memory as if it were yesterday. It seemed to me that we were somehow communicating with each other – he … 'I won't hurt you' and me … 'I won't hurt you either.'

The fox appeared to study me as closely as I studied him, and then, with a certain detached elegance, he turned and walked away, unhurriedly, not fearing anything from me as if a pact had been made. I watched as he strolled leisurely across the meadow and gradually disappeared from sight, and I lay there feeling as if it was my birthday.

Summer Snowflake | *Leucojum aestivum* | Plúirín samhraidh

Hoary
Rock-rose

WHAT ON EARTH were we to do? Pete and I felt like a right pair of eejits. We had caused the problem, but we couldn't find a way to solve it.

Spring seemed to arrive somewhat prematurely the year we went looking for **Hoary Rock-rose**. Perhaps it was too early to hope to find these little gems but we were driving through County Clare, en route from Galway to Limerick, and could never pass up the chance to spend even a few hours in the Burren. Time was limited so we made a beeline for the area where the Rock-rose was known to grow, along the Black Head road. On what can only be described as a stunning drive, the road from Ballyvaughan snakes along the flank of Gleninagh mountain towards Fanore, with Galway Bay on the right. After a few miles we passed the lighthouse at the tip of Black Head and the landscape took on a different aspect. Across the wide limestone pavement was a scatter of erratics or large boulders, some of them resembling rotten, grey, tobacco-stained molars, fissured and coloured by lichens and mosses. The land on the right dropped slowly towards the Atlantic, cleft into grykes and channels. Low-growing scrub, stunted Hawthorn bushes and Ivy were clinging on to whatever they could.

Finding a small space to park, we left the car and climbed over a five-bar metal gate in a low stone wall and set out at the usual botanist's rate, slowly ambling along a rough, meandering track. It was not long before we spotted our quarry. Perfectly beautiful, small pincushions of yellow stamens lay at the centre of each flower, surrounded by five crinkled petals, also yellow, turned back slightly. There were not many in flower – it was probably too early for these May bloomers to put on the full show, but the trailer was enough. They were enchanting. I took several photographs and, well satisfied, we headed back to the car, noticing several donkeys nosying and making their way down towards the gate. We decided it was time for a snack. Opening the car boot, Pete got out the thermos and a packet of Marietta biscuits – his favourite.

The donkeys continued their unhurried progress towards the gate. When one of them popped his head through the upper bars, Pete couldn't resist and gave him a biscuit. Shortly after that another donkey came. It too got Pete's special treatment. The third donkey was a much larger animal and when he pushed his head through the gate, he got a biscuit, from me this time. He gobbled it up very quickly. However, when he tried to remove his head, he found it was stuck fast. Somehow the bars of the gate were behind his ears and although he had managed to get his head through in the first place, now he couldn't get it back out. We felt so bad – and I'm sure he did too.

Pete tried to turn the creature's head so he could guide it through the bars, but that didn't work. Being as gentle as he could, he attempted to manipulate the donkey's large cranium sideways through the gap, so that the velvety ears wouldn't catch on the bars, but to no avail. We were in a fix and the problem wasn't going away. We got back into the car, thinking that perhaps if we removed ourselves from his view, the donkey might relax and disentangle himself without our help. If that didn't work, should we call a vet or the local Garda? Should we try to find the nearest farmhouse and see who owned the poor creature? We were feeling more than a little foolish. Then Pete came up with a bright idea. Taking the packet of biscuits, he climbed back over the wall and walked slowly around to the rear of the donkey. He rattled the packet behind the animal and took out a biscuit. The donkey's interest in another Marietta biscuit was greater than his concern for his ears and with a swift revolution of his head, he extricated it and turned around to face Pete. At this stage Pete was surrounded by the rest of the donkeys and was extremely glad that the biscuits had been in a bumper pack marked '50% EXTRA FREE'. There was one for everyone in that audience and the incident gave a whole new meaning to the phrase 'that takes the biscuit'!

Donkey

Hoary Rock-rose | *Helianthemum oelandicum* | **Grianrós liath**

WHENEVER I SEE the first **Cowslips** of the year, I imagine myself back in a field near Sandyford, County Dublin, in the mid-1950s.

It was a sunny day in late April. I was with my next-door pal and we were out cycling on our high nellies. We both had a growing curiosity about what lay the other side of a very long, very high wall and our bikes ground to a halt as we approached the imposing gates at the centre of the wall. Either side of the large gates were smaller side gates and this time – we'd tried more than once before – one of them yielded to a little pressure and – bingo – we were through, velocipedes and all.

What a sight lay before us. It was the biggest field I'd ever seen in our neighbourhood. Really large with great big trees – probably Chestnut, hindsight suggests. The grass was ankle deep, very damp and starred with bright yellow **Dandelions**. Well away from the wall and the common gaze lay an old house in an extremely dilapidated condition. It was at the end of a drive that was partly overgrown and marked out with faded, whitewashed stones, standing like small bollards at regular intervals. On either side of the field, behind ditches, the hedgerows were beginning to green, the bushy shrubs and trees giving way to splashes of golden **Gorse** here and there, with pussy willow trees making the backdrop.

On the grassy meadow was the greatest prize of all – hundreds of Cowslips. They were in such abundance – it was unbelievable how many stems held little radiating clusters of yellow flowers, carrying them above the long tongues of their green leaves. We set about picking them and when we each had a large bunch, we ran back to the bikes we had abandoned in the grass. Just as we did, we heard a creaking sound. The big gates were being opened. We froze, our Cowslips behind our backs, grasped gently but firmly and, by some instinct, hidden from sight. One man drove a pickup truck through the gates while another man closed them. As he walked towards the waiting truck, he spotted us and came over, looking extremely cross.

'What d'you think you're doing?' he barked. I recognised him as a local shopkeeper, one who was never very nice to us when we were sent for the 'messages'. I quaked and we both squeaked 'Nothing' in unison.

o Cowslips

'What have you got behind your backs?' he asked, gesturing for us to show him. We reluctantly held out the Cowslips – our Cowslips – and he snatched them from us.

'How dare you take what's not yours,' he said, 'Were you never taught not to steal?' We were both dumbstruck and made no reply. He strode over to the hedge and threw the flowers into the ditch in front of it. Then he told us to go home and not to come back again or he'd have to visit our parents. Having finished giving us this dressing-down, he went back to the truck and it rolled up the drive, passing around the side of the house and disappearing from sight.

We raced to the ditch, swiftly picking up whatever Cowslips hadn't been damaged, bringing them back to our bikes and laying them gently into the baskets on the handlebars. We pushed the bikes out through the

little gates and sped off, standing on the pedals all the way. When I got home I put my bunch of treasures into a jam jar, which I filled with water and left on a shelf in the back shed. I had plans for it.

The next day was a Sunday. I woke to the familiar clunk of the milk bottles on the front step. I was due to go to school for an extracurricular session. This was in preparation for my entry into the Father Mathew Feis, where I was to sing two songs. A pair of us had been chosen for this competition and it was taking place on Monday – the very next day. Sister Cecilia, an elderly nun who prepared pupils for music examinations, had suggested that an extra lesson might do no harm and mine was scheduled for mid-morning. Before I left home, I gathered up the Cowslips and, using a snow-white hair ribbon, I tied the stems of the flowers together, finishing with a wide bow. I laid them back in the front basket of the bike and cycled the three miles to school.

One of the younger nuns showed me into a room in the convent which I had never been in before, where Sister Cecilia was waiting. This was a bare, cold room, smelling of wax polish. Gracing two walls were pictures of Blessed Maria Goretti and, with his animals and birds, the patron saint of nature lovers, St Francis of Assisi. A large crucifix hung over the fireplace. The furniture was sparse but in the corner was an upright piano. Sister Cecilia greeted me quietly and I handed her my bunch of Cowslips – I intended this gesture to be a mark of my gratitude for her help. I wanted to give her something I thought she would appreciate – something from nature's bounty. She took the flowers and said, 'They are very nice, thank you, but you know they can't go on the altar – they're wild flowers after all.'

I was never so flattened in my life and choked back the tears I felt rising, close to the point of overflowing. But I succeeded in hiding my dismay as she put the flowers into an empty glass vase on the mantelpiece, saying she would give them water later. Then she sat back at the piano and started to play the introduction to my first song. An extremely difficult piece, it was 'Where the bee sucks, there suck I', with words by William Shakespeare and set to music by eighteenth-century composer Thomas Arne. A few of the lines in the first verse held a special significance for me.

Where the bee sucks, there suck I:
In a cowslip's bell I lie;
There I couch when owls do cry.
On the bat's back I do fly
After summer merrily.
Merrily, merrily shall I live now
Under the blossom that hangs on the bough.

When I started to sing, I could feel the pain in my freshly bruised heart, but something was being released into my voice. I soared and rose high with the notes, while the sun filled the bare room, its rays lighting the

A posy for Sister Cecilia

little 'weeds'. Perhaps it was the acoustics of the bare room, perhaps it was the hurt inside me, my beloved Cowslips slighted, becoming second-class flowers, but Maria Callas couldn't have sounded such pure, true notes.

Sister Cecilia must have noticed because, as the song ended, she said to me – and it was so out of character for her to pay any sort of compliment – 'I think if you sing like that tomorrow, you can only win first place'. Her words did absolutely nothing to mend the damage she had inflicted.

That night, my gymslip and blouse hung, ironed and ready for my appearance at the Feis. The next day, I cycled over to my schoolfriend Clare's house and together with her mother we got the bus into town. We walked along the quays to the Father Mathew Hall in good time for the Feis. I knew there was no hope whatsoever of my achieving what Sister Cecilia had predicted. Overnight I had developed what can only be described as 'a bloodshot voice'. A touch of laryngitis, maybe, or perhaps something quite different. However I tried, it was a disaster. A few notes came out, then a few squeaks and halfway through the first song, I was waved off the stage. Maria Callas was safe, and my short career as a soprano came to an end.

As for the Cowslips, I learned an early but hard lesson in sociology – all God's children are not born equal.

Cowslip | *Primula veris* | **Bainne bó bleachtáin**

Dandelion | *Taraxacum* agg. | **Caisearbhán**

We live in an age of incredibly wonderful inventions; that cannot be denied, but if you were asked what single invention you would wish to have banned from the world – forever – what would it be? I would have no hesitation in banishing from this earth that noisy, ear-splitting, destructive, nasty gadget: the strimmer. I shall tell you why.

Violets are incredibly pretty flowers and some of them have managed to elude me for far too long. The Violet most commonly found in both urban and rural habitats is the **Common Dog-violet** and it is most welcome in my garden where it grows beneath the hedges. I have also found its little cousin, **Marsh Violet**, growing, as one might suspect, in damp, swampy

Early
Dog-violet

Sweet Violet

places. And the little **Turlough** or **Fen Violet** is a rare Burren delight (see page 95). But there were two other violets, **Early Dog-violet** and **Sweet Violet**, that I had been seeking out for a very long time, to no avail. Neither of these species is scarce in Ireland; they're just not very common. Then, in the spring of 2013, my fortunes changed.

A tip-off from a botanical friend led me to an old graveyard adjoining a church in County Wexford. It was a chilly morning at the end of April and I was hoping to find an Early Dog-violet that I had heard grew abundantly in this location. There was a bank at the end of the graveyard, shaded by a canopy of sparse beech leaves – perfect textbook habitat. I mooched around in it for a while, hunting through the vegetation and leaf litter and I saw what I thought might just be the flowers in question. I think that the collective noun for Violets should be 'a confusion'. I find this genus difficult to identify and I wasn't sure whether I had unearthed the Early or the Common Dog-violet. I had to be certain and the only way was to examine the flowers through my hand lens and then relate what I saw to my wildflower guides. I went back to the car to get the bag of gear I usually carry with me, but I realised that I had left it on the kitchen table. I drove back to the house, as quickly as I legally could, snatched a quick bite of lunch and returned about an hour later.

When I got back to the graveyard, a sad sight met my eyes and I used some very unholy words – to myself, of course. In order to have the cemetery as weed-free as possible, that bane of the field-botanist, the strimmer, had been in action. The area between and around the graves was shaved almost to the earth. The person wielding the strimmer had done a very thorough job and there was neither a weed nor a blade of grass to be seen; indeed, he had even managed to strim under the trees along the banks. Nothing had escaped. I wouldn't be surprised if he had even strimmed the carpet up the centre aisle of the church in his zeal. Ironically, fresh French Marigolds had been planted in neat, measured rows on some graves. Vases of cut flowers had been settled into the earth beside other sites. Crêpe-paper flowers were scattered on some plots and there were even several wreaths of brightly coloured plastic flowers, already starting to fade. I found it hard not to rant, rave and leave the ground; I was literally hopping mad.

What I had not taken into account was that the following Sunday would be the day on which the Blessing of the Graves would take place in that particular graveyard. Many rural parishes designate a particular Sunday as the day when relatives visit the graves of their loved ones and say prayers over them. I can see that in order to cater for visitors of all abilities and lessen the risk of accidental falls, it is a good idea to have the ground as hazard-free as possible. I put a note in my next year's diary to visit again – a week or two earlier.

Another Violet caused my blood pressure to rise. Once again I got a call. 'Would you be interested in seeing some Sweet Violets'?

Would a fish swim? I was off again. This time, the flowers were growing in the ruins of an old, derelict castle and when I got there, I noticed that there were signs all over the ruins warning visitors to enter at their peril, clearly pointing out that the building could come tumbling down on them at any moment. However, Violets can't read and they had chosen to grow inside the ruins. I had to see them. I edged forwards and, bending almost double, passed under an enormous piece of granite that lay across what had probably been an entrance at some stage, many moons ago. The light was bad, the nerves were worse, and there were only a couple of flowers still looking even slightly photogenic. But I could see that they were different from any violet I had seen before. Each flower was snow-white, with a spur of deep purple. The leaves were broad, heart-shaped and downy, held on long stems. But I couldn't concentrate on the flowers, no matter how hard I tried. The remaining walls of the castle had large cracks running through them and were topped with loose masonry, perilously balanced. I don't usually suffer from camera shake but the circumstances were far from ideal. I took several mediocre frames, folded myself in two again and beat a hasty retreat. The photographs would never win prizes but they were enough to confirm the identification – for now. That's the best about field botany. There's always next year.

Common Dog-violet | *Viola riviniana* | Fanaigse

Marsh Violet | *Viola palustris* | Sailchuach chorraigh

Early Dog-violet | *Viola reichenbachiana* | Sailchuach luath

Sweet Violet | *Viola odorata* | Sailchuach chumhra

I WAS SUPPOSED to be guarding his right flank but I failed miserably and he was killed. Not just wounded but killed. Dead. I let him die. No, this is not an entry in a war diary but a day in my life as a wage slave.

They were called 'Away Days'. The intention was to bond workmates together for the glory and continued success of the company, and therefore, themselves. Team Building, Leadership, Conflict Handling, Goal Focusing and Time Management … we would learn all in one day. A wizard of a consultant who knew all about Performance Management would address us on the subject of coexistence and getting the best out of ourselves and our fellow ants. He would give us little tests to see whether we were movers or shakers, solid citizens, sheep or misfits. Then the role playing would begin and we would go back to our office desks the next day, full of zeal and game plans.

Most of us abhorred these days, even the swanky dinner in a posh hotel afterwards didn't make up for the sheer terror of being found to be a misfit and being sent to the company's equivalent of the Gulag forever.

But there I was, dressed from head to toe in a very unflattering, camouflage-style outfit – I think 'fatigues' is what they are called in army parlance. Over my face was a mask and goggles, on my head a heavy plastic helmet. I was carrying a rather nasty and unwieldy gun. I had been issued with my supply of ammunition and my role was to guard and protect my boss's right-hand side.

We had been divided into two armies, the leaders easily distinguished by their different coloured helmets. The goal was to capture a certain rocky knoll at the other side of a patch of woodland. We advanced towards our target, slowly, crouching low as we crept stealthily forwards. Rough paths criss-crossed the woods. My foot trod on a dry twig and it cracked loudly. Ouch. Our leader turned to me, gesturing. I couldn't see his face, but I didn't really need to. His body language told me he was not at all pleased. Normally, at my yearly review, he would give me 'Above Average' for Effort but I only ever got an 'Average' for Achievement. I dreaded to think what boxes he would tick next year.

It was hot and sweaty inside this horrible outfit. My hair was getting plastered to my scalp under the olive-green helmet and my deodorant had stopped working. I wondered who had last been in this boiler suit, had it even been washed since, and I really did not want to be there one little bit. This was County Wicklow after all. This was a place where I loved to walk in peace and tranquillity, whatever time of the year. This was where I would breathe in the fresh country air, deep into my lungs, and it would help to keep me sane from one weekend to the next. It never, ever let me down.

But I had to participate. There was no way out of it. Take part or else. I suppose I was lucky: I had a good job in a company that treated their employees very well. It was just this war stuff … it was definitely not for me.

We moved slowly, carefully, trying to see out through the steamed-up goggles, creeping forward quietly, the intention being to reach the knoll first and plant our flag. If necessary, we would seize or kill our foe, one by one, the prize going to the person who captured the enemy's leader. The trees were close together in this part of the wood, the vegetation quite deep on either side of the track. If we kept ourselves low, perhaps they wouldn't notice us until it was too late.

Then I saw it. Even through my fogged-up goggles I could make it out. Tucked in at the bottom of a tree, in a little hollow where a foot would never fall was an **Early-purple Orchid**. I had only encountered this magnificent wildflower once before. A few years earlier I had found one in the Burren, but never since.

o Early-purple
Orchid

Woodland in County Wicklow

Although not a rare species, it is not very common and this specimen was in absolutely perfect condition. Erect, elegant spikes bore superb magenta-purple flowers, with long, upward-pointing spurs and exquisitely decorated lips. Spotted leaves surrounded the stems emerging from the fertile woodland floor. What a wonderful surprise!

That was when my leader fell. He had been 'taken out', as they say these days. He was covered from head to toe, not in blood red but in shocking pink! I had – somehow – failed to notice that two members of the opposing paintball army had snuck up on our right. Now, how on earth did that

happen? It was just as well my face was behind a mask. I would have time to compose my countenance before it was unveiled. There would probably be a few well-chosen, possibly withering words over the posh dinner that evening, to say nothing of the next annual performance review. Not even the slightest chance of an 'Average' mark for Achievement this time. However, I now knew where an Early-purple Orchid grew in County Wicklow. I would be back.

Early-purple Orchid | *Orchis mascula* | **Magairlín meidhreach**

Seen on the wing in April

The **Holly Blue** is a small butterfly that flies in gardens, woodland and hedgerows. Its underwing has little black spots and its larval foodplants are Holly in spring, and Ivy in summer.

The female **Orange-tip** lays her eggs on plants of Cuckooflower. The male is far more eye-catching with his bright orange wing tips. He flies in damp hedgerows, meadows and gardens.

The perfectly named **Speckled Wood** is found in hedges, gardens and woodland, in the dappled light of summer, using grasses such as Yorkshire Fog as its larval foodplant. Given its preference for damp shady habitats, it is no wonder that it is Ireland's most common butterfly species.

Female Orange-tip

Holly Blue

Above: Male Orange-tip
Right: Speckled Wood

Hawthorn

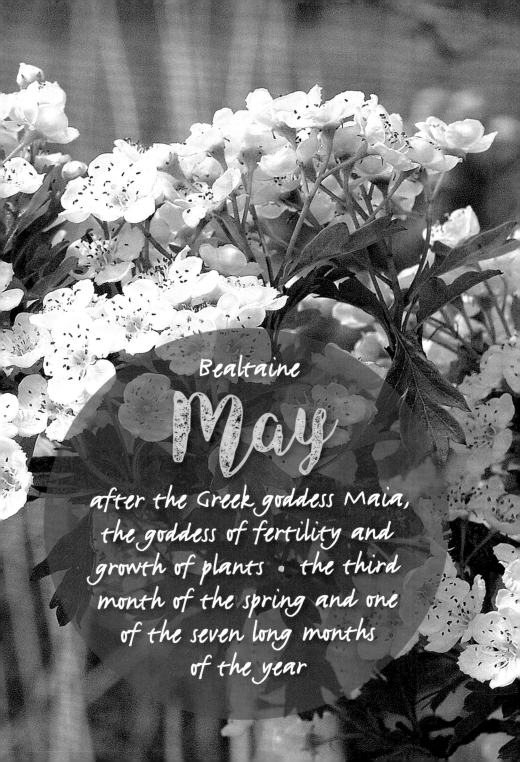

Bealtaine

May

after the Greek goddess Maia,
the goddess of fertility and
growth of plants • the third
month of the spring and one
of the seven long months
of the year

Blackbird

Thrush

'N E'ER CAST A CLOUT TILL MAY BE OUT' is an old saying over which there still seems to be some confusion. Does it mean don't shed any clothing until the month of May has ended? Or does it mean keep your winter woollies on until the May blossom is out? This would refer to the superb flowers of Hawthorn, the widespread hedgerow shrub also known as 'May bush'. I think the jury is still out on this one.

May is also the month of the dawn chorus. Although this avian concert can be heard for some time before and after May, this is the month when our feathered friends excel themselves by giving a magnificent performance of birdsong. It is a phenomenon as old as time, usually beginning after 2 a.m., and it is all about defending territory and attracting a mate, principally among woodland birds. The chorus opens just before the sun begins to rise, when one bird – often a Blackbird or Thrush – starts to sing. Slowly other voices join in, becoming progressively stronger and louder and a wonderful fusion of airs and melodies reaches a pitch. This slowly dies back as daylight arrives. It is the time when I like to make sure my bedroom window is wide open so I won't miss this marvellous event, although it is best experienced out of doors. It is the one month of the year when I never mind waking early.

Hawthorn | *Crataegus monogyna* | Sceach gheal

ONE OF THE HIGHEST passes in Ireland, at 400 metres, the Conor Pass carves its way through the breathtaking Kerry landscape.

Pete and I first experienced this stunning col or parting in the mountains, as we wove our way up through extremely rugged and steep terrain on the way from Castlegregory to Dingle. This narrow road cuts dramatically across the Dingle Peninsula, running diagonally in a north-east to south-west trajectory. Slea Head is further west again, with its silent remnants of human existence – clocháns or beehive huts. These drystone dwellings have been known in Kerry since the twelfth century, some linked together in compounds, others used by monks seeking tranquillity and solitude, such as those on Skellig Michael.

On either side of the Conor Pass, a thick blanket of peat bog clothes the hillsides. Sedges and rushes grow in abundance. The diminished soil, a legacy of the scouring action of the last Ice Age, was depleted of many nutrients, thus dictating the type of plants capable of living on it. Corries or coums – shallow lakes caused as heavy ice deposits gouged them out – gave witness to the glacial meltwater's action. Small, stone-walled fields bore evidence of human activities.

Clochán on Slea Head, County Kerry

St Patrick's-
cabbage

The road grew narrower as we ascended, sharp cliff faces bordering the steep, narrowing road. Pete had drawn the short straw and was doing the driving while I gazed, marvelling at this incredible part of Kerry. I asked him to stop, if it was possible; I had spotted a plant growing in a crevice and really wanted to have a closer look. The fissures in this wild rockery contained an abundance of plants and I knew, quite quickly, that I had spotted **St Patrick's-Cabbage**. Pete found a little lay-by and I took a few photographs. Images I had previously taken of this species had not been good. I was more than pleased.

However, this was not the species I was hunting. My holy grail on this occasion was **Large-flowered Butterwort.**

We continued along the ever-tapering route to the top, and suddenly, there they were – up the steep, rock-strewn ground at the edge of the road – a small group of plants bearing the most unimaginably stunning purple flowers. At the base of each plant was a starry arrangement of pale green leaves, covered in a sticky, flypaper-like substance, with several insects being slowly digested by the plant. The paucity of nutrients in the soil is the reason why this carnivorous species, along with other Butterworts and the Sundews (see January) evolved this method of getting nutrition. But it is the flowers that are the most attractive, intriguing and utterly beautiful parts of the plant. Held with a lofty elegance at the top of erect stems were purple or deep-violet funnel-shaped flowers. Each of these was decorated with purple streaks running along a white strip and

Large-flowered Butterwort

this led through the three-lobed lower lip into the throat of the flower. A tangle of tiny, purple spikes carpeted this white strip and the result of all of these details was an absolutely amazing flower – it had to be seen to be believed.

I was thrilled with the find but my roll of film was nearly finished. This was in pre-digital days and I had just three frames left – and the light was appalling. I knew the photographs would never be any good. For one reason or another, it was to be more than thirty years before I saw those superb flowers again. Fast-forward to 2011 and a further hunt for Large-flowered Butterwort.

If you look at a distribution map for this species, you'll see that in Ireland it is almost completely confined to County Kerry and west Cork. However, there are two little dots – each representing a verified record – which locate this species in the Burren region of County Clare. I just needed to be there at the right time – during May or, at a pinch and with a lot of luck, early June.

Late June was the best we could manage but, full of optimism, we took a trip there and, joining a botanist friend, Paul Green, we decided to see if we might be lucky. Paul is one of the most gifted, helpful and generous people I know. He has shared an enormous amount of his botanical knowledge with me over the years and I hope that even a small percentage has taken root.

All the collective wisdom said that it was probably too late in the month, but hope springs eternal in a flower-hunter's breast. June had already been exceedingly wet and that day was no exception. As we slogged along the sodden uphill track, the rain got heavier and heavier. Stubbornly, I just knew I could not turn back before seeing whether the flowers were still in bloom. Our waterproofs were not living up to their name but there was a doggedness about us and I did so want to see the species again. We found them, but they were so far past their best that I didn't take a single photograph. They were tired, tattered and torn, and had begun the serious work of setting seed.

A little trickle of water was finding its way down my back – and beyond – and I was feeling very bad for having suggested the expedition in the first place. And then … through the grey, damp gloom of the day, my eyes spotted a strange sight, one I had never seen before. I grabbed Paul's arm and he also stopped in his tracks. It was an extremely rare variation of the **Bee Orchid**, the species that bears such a resemblance to a real bee that the insects try to make love to it.

Bee Orchids and **Fly Orchids** share the same mechanism for ensuring the survival of their species. These plants emit a scent that, together with their appearance, attracts the appropriate insect. While the little creature tries to mate with the flower, pollen that has been held above the centre of the flower in two 'pollinia' or pockets, rubs off onto the insect's body. Then, his romantic intentions thwarted, the frustrated little creature flies away and lands on the next plant to be made a fool of once again. This means that the pollen on his body is transferred to the pollinia of the second plant, thus guaranteeing further generations of these species. Bees and flies are fooled by this cruel deception which is called 'pseudocopulation'.

Pete held our large black umbrella over me and the plant while I crouched down and took a few photographs of this rare white Bee Orchid. The light was woeful but we were now in the digital age. The results were enough to make a

Bee
Orchid

White Bee
Orchid

positive identification. There is one main difference between this variant and the 'ordinary' Bee Orchid. In this specimen the usual three spreading pink sepals above and beside the furry, bee-like lower lip were replaced by three white sepals. Personally I prefer the standard version but it was extremely exciting to see this rarity. Later I found that it was only the second record of this particular specimen in Ireland. What a find!

But I still hadn't got a decent photograph of Large-flowered Butterwort.

Then, in late May 2012, we went for a walk with other members of Burrenbeo, a community-based charity working for the good of biodiversity and the environment in County Clare. As we wandered along slowly, we came upon a superb colony of Large-flowered Butterwort on the hillside we had visited the previous year. Just as I knelt down with the camera, a call went up from the leader of the walk: 'Bulls in the field! Everybody out!' Such a scatter – suddenly the slow pace of the afternoon changed and near Olympic speeds were reached. However, I now knew that the plants were there and in perfect condition this time, so the following day, taking my courage in my hands and posting Pete as lookout – all he was short of was a matador's cape – I spent at least an hour in the company of these handsome flowers.

No photograph could ever do them justice but I tried to convey some of their elegance, their graceful shape and their deep purple hue. Even though these flesh-eating plants devour unfortunate little insects, I can forgive them. They have to survive, as do we, by getting their nutritional life force from wherever they can.

St Patrick's-cabbage | *Saxifraga spathularis* | **Cabáiste mhadra rua**

Bee Orchid | *Ophrys apifera* | **Magairlín na mbeach**

Bee Orchid – white version | *Ophrys apifera* var. *flavescens*

Large-flowered Butterwort | *Pinguicula grandiflora* | **Leith uisce**

Graveyard

REPUTED TO BE the tree from which Judas hanged himself, **Elder** has far more pleasant connections for me.

Some years ago I was offered a glass of cordial made from the creamy, frothy flowerheads of this tree and from that time on I have been hooked. It is really tasty and refreshing, and is also quite straightforward to make. All you have to be sure of is that the Elder tree is well away from any source of pollution. My favourite Elder tree is in an old disused graveyard and is far away from any traffic/car fumes. Interestingly, this species was often planted in cemeteries to ward off evil spirits.

Elderflower Cordial

Gather the heads of flowers on a dry, sunny day as it is the pollen which gives the flavour. No need to wash them, just shake out any unwanted travellers and snip the flowers off the larger stalks into a big bowl – I use twenty heads of fresh Elderflowers.

Warm 1.5 litres/2½ pints of water in a large saucepan and add in 2.5kg/5½lb of white sugar, dissolving it slowly over a low heat, then pour the liquid over the Elderflowers. I also add two large or three small, thinly sliced, unwaxed lemons and 60g/2oz of citric acid (which acts as a preservative). Then cover the bowl with cling film and leave it for two days, giving it the odd stir. The aroma in the entire house is wonderful.

After two days, uncover the brew and strain it through muslin into another large bowl. Then strain it back into the first bowl (rinsed) just in case you've missed anything. Finally, pour it into clean bottles and refrigerate. The cordial keeps for about six weeks, if it's let, or you can use clean plastic bottles and freeze it but be sure not to fill the bottles too full, leaving room for expansion in the freezer.

It is at its best served with sparkling water – six or seven parts water to one part cordial – and I like it served with shortbread on a sunny summer afternoon. Enjoy!

Elder | *Sambucus nigra* | Trom

Omey Island, County Galway

As THE MOURNERS started to take their leave, peeling away into smaller clusters, slowly and tenderly sharing memories, I took my place towards the outside of the group. I was on Omey Island on a warm May day with Angela, who was saying farewell to her old friend Mary.

Angela was one of those people who brought out the best in others. It was a rare gift. She lived a stone's throw from the sea in Cleggan, County Galway, and I loved to visit her whenever I could, always coming away renewed and refreshed, and not purely from the Atlantic air.

She had phoned me a couple of days earlier to tell me that Mary had died after a long illness. She was to be buried on Omey Island. Knowing I had been fond of Mary, Angela asked if I would like to come with her to the funeral. I travelled over the next day. I could never turn down the opportunity to visit Angela and her part of the world, even though it was for a funeral.

I hate rushing so gave myself plenty of time, having, of course, packed my camera in the hopes of seeing the odd wildflower or two over in the west. The last part of the journey took me from Clifden to Cleggan, the tarred road threading its way across rough, mossy-coloured bogland and, as it rose and fell, it bumped and jolted every bone in my body and every loose screw in the old Renault 4L. I had to drive quite slowly but didn't mind in the least. It gave me the chance to take the odd sideways glance at the vegetation on the bog while still keeping the car on a reasonably straight path. I spotted the occasional blob of pink here and there and I decided that the 4L needed to take a break. We slowly came to a halt at the side of the road between two small stooks of cut turf.

The Atlantic breeze was more of a gale, catching the car door – and me – by surprise. As I made my way across the uneven ground, the plants danced and tossed about wildly. Those blobs of pink came into focus and I could see that they were **Common Spotted-orchids**. Extremely delicate flowers, their lower lips were full of furbelows and frills, decorated with the most intricate designs imaginable of squiggles, dots and loops. I wanted to photograph them so I knelt down on the soggy ground, but the westerly wind was relentless. One specimen was growing in a cutting below where, I thought, it would perhaps be sheltered, unaffected by the gale. I tried to crouch near enough to get a good close-up of the flower but no matter how I twisted and turned, my own faint shadow lay across the flower.

I have always kept a firm rule-of-thumb: I never – ever – pick wildflowers in order to photograph them unless there are simply hundreds of them about. I almost always take my photographs of flowers where they grow. But particularly in the case of wild orchids, I could never pick one. It can take seven or eight years for wild orchid seeds to germinate. These seeds, tiny blueprints for the next generation, are amongst the smallest in the plant kingdom. Scattered by the wind, their germination relies totally on the presence of a specific fungus in the soil, which the orchid exploits for nutrients. I was not going to pick one in order to get a better photograph – to do so would be a 'mortaller' (for those who did not come through the Roman Catholic schooling system in 1950s Dublin, this was our shorthand for a 'mortal sin'). I just took a few frames – this was in the days of film photography – and then I drove straight to Angela's where I got the usual warm welcome from her and her exuberant Golden Retriever, Lassie.

The funeral was to take place the following afternoon. Omey Island is a small island, only accessible at low tide. To get there, we initially travelled along the wild and superb Aughrus Peninsula and on to the village of Claddaghduff. From there, the road descended onto a flat stretch of hard sand. A line of signposts indicated the route across the 600-metre channel onto the island. Once home to nearly 300 people, it is now deserted for most of the year. Funerals to Omey Island's ancient graveyard,

Common
Spotted-orchid

Signs pointing the way to Omey Island at low tide

Ula Bhreandain, have to be scheduled in accordance with the tide tables which was why this was an afternoon funeral. At high-water mark, a car would be covered by the tide.

Angela, suspecting that I might be just a little bit nervous of taking the car across this causeway, assured me it was perfectly safe to drive over the wet strand. The tyre marks of earlier vehicles could be seen, a few inches of seawater washing over them. I decided to travel hopefully: if the hearse could manage, then so would we. As we drew closer to the low-lying island, Angela pointed out the old cemetery, clearly visible on our right. We arrived on firmer land, our tyres scrunching comfortingly on the mixture of dry sand and broken seashells covering the ground. There were dozens of other cars – Mary had been a much-loved lady.

The air smelled of seaweed. I inhaled, deeply. We followed a rough, trodden trail across the close-cropped turf. Hardly stirring a hair on the bare-headed congregation, the wind had died since the previous day, contributing a respectful stillness as we stood and listened to the priest's words of departure for Mary and comfort for those left behind. The raw, stark, grey call of the gulls was the only other sound. The tombstones bore witness to the centuries of life on the island, some little more than plain granite rocks, others more formal, engraved words still visible on their leeward side. It was a place of tranquillity and reflection. I felt distinctly moved, far beyond what I would have expected. Unwept tears, previously held back, waiting to be shed for others long departed, began to rise. My throat ached as I swallowed them back. My world stood still, and then the moment passed.

I looked at the untrodden, grassy expanse leading towards the centre of the island. Walking slowly, composing myself, I picked my way through the grass, between rabbit burrows and some pinkish granite boulders, scattered erratically across the turf. Then I saw it. Just one absolutely perfect Spotted-orchid. Standing still as a statue, posing for a non-existent camera, it mocked my presence. Even at such an emotional moment, I could see the irony.

After Angela had taken her leave of the funeral party, we returned safely across the sand. We were both tired and went to bed quite early. I slept soundly.

Next morning, I was surprised to see how late it was when I awoke and, somewhat apologetically, went down to the kitchen to see if Angela was around. She was. She stood beside the kitchen table with the widest smile I have ever seen on her face. In the centre of the shiny, polished table, on a circular doily of white crochet, stood a crystal vase containing at least twenty-four Common Spotted-orchids.

'After all you did yesterday, I knew you weren't happy driving across the sand, so I picked these flowers to say "Thank you" – I know you love wildflowers. These were growing behind the house in an old meadow I rarely go into, it's so wet and useless, and I thought this was a special occasion. They're for you.'

What could I say? Those Orchids probably took several years to get to the flowering stage and they had not even been given the chance to make seeds for future generations before being plucked. That was what my head told me, but my heart told me otherwise. Angela had picked the flowers for me with total innocence and a pure heart; I could only hug her and say a great big 'Thank you'. So by the light in her bay window, away from the Atlantic wind, I took my close-ups of the Common Spotted-orchids and my rule-of-thumb remained intact.

Common Spotted-orchid | *Dactylorhiza fuchsii* | Nuacht bhallach

o Dropwort

WET PLACES HAVE their attractions for 'citizen scientists' but my favourite
region in Ireland is the one place I never think of as having much wetland.
It is the Burren. Think of those limestone hills, gently terraced with
fissured cliffs and the image is of dry places. The only permanent surface
watercourse is the Caher River, which flows to the sea close to Fanore. But
then there is a particularly Irish phenomenon – the turlough or *tuar lach*,
meaning dry place – a singular wonder which I first came across back in
the 1980s.

Pete and I were staying in Ballyvaughan, along with our friends Tony
and Anne. Their intention was to do a bit of walking in an area new to
them. Pete wanted to do a spot of birdwatching, and my plan was to
try to locate two wildflower species I'd never seen before – **Dropwort**
and **Lesser Meadow-rue**. Dropwort is a rare, native perennial closely
related to Meadowsweet but far and away prettier. It has clusters of six-
petalled white flowers, each with a mass of long, creamy-white stamens
at its centre. What adds beauty to an already stunning picture is the deep
pink of the unopened flower buds, along the stem above those flowers
already blooming. A truly designer species, its long leaves are feathery and

Lesser Meadow-rue

shiny with leaflets, both large and very small, alternating along a central stem. I located it growing in a meadow on Slieve Carron in the north-east of the Burren. Lesser Meadow-rue is quite different. It bears loose panicles of tiny, petalless flowers whose drooping yellow and purple stamens seem to quiver in the Burren air. It is a plant usually noticed for its pretty foliage, which is not unlike that of **Maidenhair Fern**. It was growing in an area of limestone close to Mullaghmore when I found it a few days into our holiday.

We had been given permission to use an old cottage as our accommodation, free of charge as none of us was in a position to pay for even one-star accommodation. The cottage had seen better days, but it was a dry roof over our heads and we were most grateful to the friend of a friend who kindly let us

Maidenhair Fern

Loch Gealáin and Mullaghmore Mountain, County Clare

stay there. We arrived late on a Friday evening and on our way down to the small loo behind the cottage we noticed that over the boundary wall was a large field. We ate our supper and had an early night, snuggling into our sleeping bags, listening to very heavy rain falling during the night. Imagine our surprise the next morning when the field behind the cottage had completely vanished under a wide, field-sized lake. It was our first experience of a turlough.

A characteristic of the Burren – and a couple of other locations in Ireland where limestone exists – the turlough is a shallow lake which disappears in dry weather and reappears after extremely heavy rainfall. As limestone can be eroded by rainwater, its fissures and cracks widen over time until almost all of the rain finds it way underground. Then, in times of high precipitation, this groundwater rises, emerging through the swallow holes on the floor of the turlough, creating a temporary lake that gradually drains away, usually through the same aperture. Since that first encounter with a turlough, we have even seen the phenomen of water springing out from the Burren hillsides and cascading down as temporary 'pop-up' waterfalls.

Turloughs can range in size from small lakes to more extensive bodies of water, such as Loch Gealáin, which is an incredibly clear, sparkling body of fluctuating water beside Mullaghmore. Growing in separate bands around the margins of this particular turlough are many different types of vegetation. **Shrubby Cinquefoil**, a bushy little species with bright yellow, five-petalled flowers and silvery green foliage, is found at the higher level of flooding. Growing close to the Burren's turloughs are two more distinctive species, **Turlough** or **Fen Violet** and **Turlough Dandelion**. This Violet is a beautiful blue member of the Viola family, which can be identified mainly by its leaves: they are long and not heart-shaped like those of the

shrubby Cinquefoil

Turlough or Fen Violet

Turlough
Dandelion

Common Dog-violet. Turlough Dandelion is quite unique, too, with reddish stems and long, narrow leaves, not a bit like the usual deeply toothed leaves on the more commonly found Dandelions. However, there is one outstanding species that grows beside Loch Gealáin and it is well worth searching for in late May particularly. It is commonly known as **Flecked Marsh-orchid**, scientifically named *Dactylorhiza incarnata* subspecies *cruenta*. This was first shown to me in 2010 by Dr Matthew Jebb, then Taxonomist and now Director of the National Botanic Gardens in Dublin. I was lucky enough to be in the Burren for one of his walks, which was a real treat. His abundance of knowledge is always dispensed in an accessible manner and I have had cause to be extremely grateful for his generous help on numerous occasions. When I examined this amazing species, I was completely bowled over by its superb design. Not only was each mauve flower decorated with deep purple lines and loops, but the bracts between each individual flower in the spike were adorned with browny-purple smudges and spots. Then I looked at the leaves and they were also dotted, on both sides, with patterns on the upper side of the leaves quite different from those on the lower side. The plants were scattered, here and there, between the limestone slabs that bordered the turlough, and I think they must be one of the most handsome flowers I have ever seen.

Dropwort | *Filipendula vulgaris* | Lus braonach

Lesser Meadow-rue | *Thalictrum minus* | Rú Léana Beag

Shrubby Cinquefoil | *Potentilla fruticosa* | Tor cúigmhéarach

Turlough or Fen Violet | *Viola persicifolia* | Sailchuach uisce

Turlough Dandelion | *Taraxacum palustre* | Caisearbhán

Flecked Marsh-orchid | *Dactylorhiza incarnata* ssp. *cruenta* | Magairlín craorag

Flecked
Marsh-
orchid

MAY 97

It CAN KILL a chicken – there's a clue in the name – but it is so, so beautiful. It is **Henbane**.

Wildflowers can suffer a precarious existence. We hear depressing accounts of habitat loss causing the decline of species in the wider sense and I could recount many incidents where a particular species of wildflower has negatively experienced the human hand. One such species is Henbane.

Henbane is a remarkable wildflower. It has a most unpleasant, heavy, nauseating smell that can cause dizziness and which gives it another common name, Stinking Nightshade. Ingesting Henbane can lead to hallucinations and convulsions and it is toxic to most animals, its consumption being sometimes fatal. Now only occasionally found in Ireland, all parts of the plant are known to be lethal. It is one of several poisons suspected of being used by Hamlet's uncle, Claudius, to murder Hamlet's father. In his ghostly visit to his son, he tells Hamlet how he met his death:

Sleeping within my orchard,
My custom always of the afternoon,
Upon my secure hour thy uncle stole,
With juice of cursed hebenon in a vial,
And in the porches of my ears did pour
The leperous distilment;

Perhaps that 'leperous distilment' of 'cursed hebenon' originated in the cells of a Henbane plant.

I have seen the flowers of Henbane only once, but I can remember them vividly; they were simply magnificent. The creamy flowers were decorated with intricate, dark purple-brown lines that gradually merged together and led into a deep, brown throat. Favouring a dry, sandy habitat, this species tends to grow in coastal grassland – precisely where I saw it. On a botanical field trip the previous year, Paul Green had pointed out the rosette of leaves indicating that the plant was in the first year of its life. Henbane being a biennial, I expected to see its flowers the following year. I returned to

the spot the following May, 2011, and was thrilled to see and photograph them. In 2012 and 2013, I sought them again, hoping their scattered seeds would generate in the same location, and was over the moon when I saw what I took to be their rosette in late 2013.

The following spring, I returned to see how the plant was progressing and found that although it was growing well, it was nowhere near flowering; it was much too early. About four weeks later I went back, hoping it would be starting to bloom.

Imagine my horror when I saw that instead of the plant there was a large, freshly dug hole in the field – the plant was nowhere to be seen. My heart sank. I can only presume that the Henbane had been identified by someone who, knowing its potential dark side, informed the people living locally. Who can blame anybody for wishing to remove a source of danger to either people or animals, cattle in particular, as the spot was adjacent to grazing land? I have to try to see it from their point of view, but it highlights the difficulties of nature and man trying to live together, cheek by jowl.

Henbane | *Hyoscyamus niger* | Gafann

Narrow-leaved
Helleborine

Then there are some plants that just like to live dangerously. They put themselves in the wrong places and there is little that can be done to help them when this happens. Take, for instance, the beautiful, snowy-white **Narrow-leaved Helleborine,** which a friend told me was growing on a roadside in County Galway. His excellent directions led me to several plants between the road and the edge of a deciduous wood. This was a rare species I had never seen before, with spikes of snow-white flowers that were in extremely good order. There were no blemishes or burnt spots, which can sometimes ruin a photograph. These members of the Orchid family only grow in a few locations around Ireland so I knew how lucky I was. As it happened, my friend was to come along the same road the next day and I texted him, thanking him for his clear directions. He was delighted as he had not seen them that year and renewing acquaintance with a rare species is always very special.

The next evening, I received a text from him saying 'Saw remains of flowers. Lorry wheel marks. Flowers flattened. Dead'. It was a narrow country road and if two vehicles were to meet, at least one of them would have to go up on the verge.

On the positive side, there was once a very large colony of **Pyramidal Orchid** growing on an embankment near what was known in the 1960s as 'The Big Tree' in Loughlinstown, County Dublin. This referred to a large, mature Chestnut tree that stood at the centre of one of Ireland's first dual carriageways, on the main road connecting Dublin with County Wicklow. The plants remained there until the early years of the new millennium when the road was upgraded with a very elaborate junction, complete with flyover. However, before the roadworks took place, those Orchids – and large amounts of the soil beneath them – were carefully lifted from the embankment and transferred to a place of safety on another part of our road network. Happily, this type of support for our biodiversity is now becoming more commonplace.

Recently, due to the construction of another motorway near Ardrahan in County Galway, large swathes

Pyramidal
Orchid

Early-purple Orchids at the National Botanic Gardens, Glasnevin

of wildflowers, including nine species of Orchids, were threatened with destruction but, before the preliminary work of clearing the site had begun, they were removed by volunteers and planted elsewhere in safe, secure and suitable locations. Some were planted near Oranmore, also in County Galway, while others are now growing in the wildflower plots at the National Botanic Gardens in Glasnevin, County Dublin.

Narrow-leaved Helleborine | *Cephalanthera longifolia* | Cuaichín caol

Pyramidal Orchid | *Anacamptis pyramidalis* | Magairlín na stuaice

Early-purple Orchid | *Orchis mascula* | Magairlín meidhreach

Male Eider Duck

As WE WALKED along the beach at Church Bay, we listened to the calm, soothing sound of the tide lapping on the sand at the water's edge. Then a second sound, quite different, soft and gently humorous.

It was the call of Common Eider ducks, their rich cooing and murmuring quite unmistakeable. Making the sound to attract a female, the stunning male raises his head with each '*coo*', pointing his beak skywards. There were several of these splendid creatures sailing along the shiny water, little bow waves rolling across their wide breasts.

True sea ducks, Eiders spend most of their lives on the ocean's surface. They are such handsome birds, both male and female, but the male's spectacular plumage is outstanding. It is mainly black and white, with pale green on the sides of his neck and a rosy hue on his chest. His attire is definitely the formal dress suit. The female's is more cryptic. She is a duller, less dramatic creature with brown plumage and, like the male, she has a wedge-shaped beak. She doesn't feel the need to attract attention – her child-minding role means she needs to keep a far lower profile than he does, keeping the ducklings safe from predators rather than cutting a stylish dash.

We were visiting Rathlin Island, a small, boomerang-shaped island lying 10 kilometres off the north Antrim coast. Although tourism is now the mainstay of the island's income, at the eastern end of Church Bay there is evidence of a former industry in the ruins of a building once used for drying and burning seaweed.

In the eighteenth and nineteenth centuries, Rathlin was a major centre for the production of kelp. Seaweed was gathered and burned for use as a fertiliser and also in various chemical processes, creating a major means of support for many of the islanders. However, after a change in import duty, kelp from Spain became a more viable purchase for many industries. As a result, this business on Rathlin, and on the west coast of Scotland, collapsed in the middle of the nineteenth century, causing great hardship.

These days, a fast ferry service connects Rathlin with Ballycastle. Superb views of Fair Head and beyond, to the Mull of Kintyre, make this a most memorable trip in itself. If you are lucky, you might see Gannets diving for their food in this passage, the Sea of Moyle.

Pete and I first visited the island in May 2011, making landfall in the early evening, the low rays of the sun casting a golden haze. The cooing of Eiders accompanied us to our accommodation close to the arrival point of the ferry in Church Bay. Seals were sitting on the rocks beside the bay, watching us with a lazy disdain, their young tumbling and playing in the shallow water close to the shore.

My mission was to find **Pyramidal Bugle**. This is an extremely rare and protected plant species known to grow on Rathlin and in the Burren. Whilst we love the Burren, we always had a wish to visit Rathlin, as much to see the island as the bird species that we don't often see near Dublin, like Eiders and Red-breasted Mergansers. The Pyramidal Bugle also gave us an excuse to make this trip. With the help of local knowledge we located it, almost past its best and not sufficiently fresh for a really good photograph – dear me, we would have to come back.

Pyramidal Bugle is closely related to another native wildflower, the woodland species **Bugle**, which is commonly found throughout Ireland. Whereas Bugle is a loose spike of blue-violet flowers growing to about 30 centimetres tall, Pyramidal Bugle is a short, compressed, cone-shaped spike of only 10 centimetres, its darker, purple flowers almost hidden between downy leaves.

Bugle

Pyramidal
Bugle

Rathlin Island lake

Rare but by no means dramatic, which is frequently the case with these scarce treasures.

There is so much I could say about Rathlin Island, which we visited again in 2016. It is the seabirds that made the most lasting impression. Between our trips, the Seabird Centre on the western end of the island was refurbished. This is an excellent facility where colonies of Puffin, Fulmar, Guillemot and Razorbill can be viewed as they nest in every nook and cranny on the crowded sea stacks opposite the Royal Society for the Protection of Birds' (RSPB) viewing platform. They make a wonderful spectacle and sound, tumbling from their perches on the sheer cliffs, wheeling and crying into the wind.

The Puffins are probably the main attraction for the wildlife-loving tourists who visit Rathlin. So many words could be used to describe them – I found them comical, cute and most endearing. In the five years between our visits, there has been

Puffins

sea stack on Rathlin Island as seen from RSPB's viewing platform

spring squill

a continued drop in Puffin numbers, which is a major cause for concern. This decline is possibly due to the diminution of an important source of food for them, sand eels, which could be down to commercial fishing – sand eels are used to produce feed for salmon farms. On our 2011 visit, we saw dozens of these birds on several levels of the cliffs opposite the observation centre. In 2016, we could only count seven of them, way down at sea level. They are now on the RSPB's Red list, meaning they are birds of highest conservation concern, their future being uncertain.

During our second visit, we came across many other bird species such as Greylag Geese, Coot and Tufted Ducks, feeding in reedbeds surrounding the gleaming waters of one of the island's small lakes. We were also reassured to see that the Pyramidal Bugle was surviving. Another species we spotted was **Spring Squill**, a small native plant, which was scattered sparsely, like so many

Bogbean

pale blue stars, across the short turf. Confined to only a few spots in northern and eastern coastal regions, it is always a delight to come across.

Rathlin is an incredibly peaceful island and it offers a tremendous feeling of serenity. Depending on the time of year, there are wonderful meadows of wildflowers, including carpets of **Common Spotted-orchids**. Its small, natural lakes are ringed by bulrushes and reeds and are home to large swathes of the extremely attractive wetland plant, **Bogbean**. Walking is relatively easy, apart from a few steep rises in the road to the west. To the south-east lies Roonivoolin where you might be lucky enough to see Snipe or a handsome Irish Hare. We spotted three of these mammals one evening, the light catching their russet coats as they capered across a small field.

Hare

I loved every minute of the time spent on Rathlin and remember it with nothing but pleasure. Sometimes it's the sound of the Eiders cooing or the languid regard of the seals on the offshore rocks; sometimes it's the smell of the seaweed or maybe the feeling of the fine, soft sand on the beach, trickling through my fingers. Other times it's the crisp, cool feel of the grass under my hands, while I sit contemplating nothing in particular but gazing into the distance, feeling a wider connection to the creatures that are at home in Rathlin. I will be back.

Pyramidal Bugle | *Ajuga pyramidalis* | Glasair bheannach

Bugle | *Ajuga reptans* | Glasair choille

Spring Squill | *Scilla verna* | Sciolla earraigh

Bogbean | *Menyanthes trifoliata* | Báchrán

LIFE WAS ANYTHING but easy and two very hard blows caused us to wonder if we could continue to keep our ship afloat for much longer.

It was tough in Ireland if you were trying to run a small business in the late 1970s and early '80s. Pete and I had started up a craft-based company in 1973 and it was moderately successful. We designed and manufactured wall hangings and decorative panels in various different types of fabric and we also undertook individual commissions, such as coats of arms and advertising banners. Our customers were many and varied, among them large and small concerns – both at home and abroad – and tourist-based companies. We both enjoyed the work, which called for a degree of creativity as well as a little bit of business acumen. At the same time, we managed to keep a roof over our heads, paying the mortgage in those demanding years when interest rates soared into the mid-teens. However, by 1979, maintaining the business as a profitable enterprise was becoming a struggle.

The 1970s was a period of high inflation, rising to 21 per cent in 1975. In one decade (1973–83) oil prices more than quadrupled. The crises in the Middle East triggered not only raised prices, but in May 1979 the fuel shortage caused long, fractious queues at petrol stations all around the country. To this problem was added massive disruption of deliveries when an eighteen-week strike was held by postal workers. This seriously affected distribution of goods. Coupled with the petrol shortage, it hit us badly during the summer months when our business should have been at its peak.

The year 1979 was a strange one for Ireland and we were not the only people to suffer the slings and arrows of a mixture of outrageous fortune and worse – bad intentions. The year had started with the deaths of fifty people in the explosion of the oil tanker *Betelgeuse* at Whiddy Island in Bantry Bay, County Cork. This was to be the worst disaster in Ireland's marine history. Then, on a warm summer day in August, Lord Louis Mountbatten and three others were killed when their fishing boat was blown up by the IRA off Mullaghmore in County Sligo. On the very

Bloody
Crane's-bill

same day, eighteen British soldiers were killed in another bomb attack in Warrenpoint, County Down.

This was a bleak period when the disastrous effects of bad economic planning and political instability were widespread. Our business also began to suffer seriously. Goods were not getting to customers, either in or out of Ireland, but at least there was some hope of our delivering them to Irish addresses. Pete had a large workload with

Petra at thirteen

some new designs to be drawn up, so I decided to head to the west of the country with a carful of orders. Our daughter, Petra, asked if could she come with me – nothing could have made me happier. She was at the stage where young girls are leaving behind their ballet shoes and roller skates, preparing to dip their toes into the moody waters of adolescence. I was delighted to have her with me.

To lower our fuel consumption we had recently downsized the car and it was chock-a-block with parcels as we left Dublin. The first scheduled stop was to be Maam Cross in County Galway but our brand-new car decided otherwise. On its maiden voyage across the central plain of Ireland it did an embarrassingly accurate impression of a steam engine in the narrowest part of Athlone's main street, its radiator showering clouds of vapour and hot water into the street. A faulty thermostat, the man at the local garage said, fixing it with a screwdriver and a smile.

'No charge', he said, 'we like helping Dubs in distress.'

After Maam Cross we drove west over the twisting, bumpy road to Cleggan, where we enjoyed the warm hospitality of our friend Angela. Next morning, we managed to top up our petrol tank in Kinvara and reckoned there was enough to get us home. Ennis was the next port of call, but rather than go directly, we decided to take a little detour through the Burren. For Petra, this would be the first of many visits. The day was beginning to get brighter, the car windows were wound right down and, in tune with the mood, the radio played Gloria Gaynor serenading us with 'I will survive'. At the tops of our voices we competed with her and won.

The limestone hills of the Burren were lit by a pearly glow, each terrace outlined with a side light that accentuated the cliffs and vertical clefts. The Hawthorn trees, laden with creamy-white clusters of flowers, were in full bloom and scattered sparsely across the stony pavement. We stopped just short of the lighthouse on Black Head. Petra wanted to see, up close, what was so special about the Burren's flowers. She climbed over a low stone wall and as she steadied herself, she exclaimed, 'Mum, this is like stepping into someone's garden'. She delicately picked her way across the grassy turf and the limestone, not wanting to step on any of the plants, just as if this was a formal garden. I was impressed by the care she took. Rough lines of grassy soil between the slabs were home to an abundance of **Spotted-orchids** of all hues from snow-white to dark lilac; **Bloody Crane's-bill** (see page 111), emerged here and there from the rough grykes, scattering

O'Kelly's spotted orchid

splashes of magenta across the landscape, and then Petra saw what she reckons is the most striking Burren flower of all, **Mountain Avens**. As you might guess from its scientific name, *Dryas octopetala,* it bears flowers with eight petals, although occasionally you might find one that can't count. These snow-white petals surround a busy circle of golden stamens. Small evergreen leaves crowd together, each resembling a miniature oak leaf, the underside covered in tiny, soft, silvery hairs. Part of the arctic/alpine element

Mountain Avens

of the fascinating Burren flora, Mountain Avens also flourishes in the Arctic and the mountains of Europe and is the national emblem of Iceland. Petra crouched over it and looked and looked and looked. She just loved it.

We have returned to the Burren many times since that visit and found its magnificent treasures in abundance. But whenever I see Mountain Avens, it brings back to me Petra's feeling of awe and respect for this species and for its environment. I recall with intense pleasure the mood that was lifted sky high by a little girl that day in 1979.

O'Kelly's Spotted-orchid | *Dactylorhiza fuchsii* var. *okellyi* | Nuacht bhallach Uí Ceallaigh

Bloody Crane's-bill | *Geranium sanguineum* | Crobh dearg

Mountain Avens | *Dryas octopetala* | Leaithín

The **Small Heath**, seen (facing page) on Eyebright, flies over grassland and dunes, favouring grasses as its larval foodplant.

The **Cryptic Wood White**, pictured below on Selfheal, can be seen in rough grasslands, road verges and hedgerows. Vetches are its larval foodplant.

The **Common Blue**, a small butterfly, is found in meadows and coastal grassland. The female lays her eggs on Bird's-foot-trefoil. The male (seen left) is very blue but the female is more cryptically coloured, underwings of both are highly decorated.

The **Clouded Yellow** is a migrant whose preferred habitat is in coastal areas of the east and south. Eggs are laid on clovers and other members of the Pea family. Seen here feeding on Sea Rocket, it is unmistakeable with a white spot on the hind wing.

Cryptic Wood White

Male and Female
Common Blues

Above: Clouded Yellow

Left: Small Heath

Large-flowered
Evening-
primrose

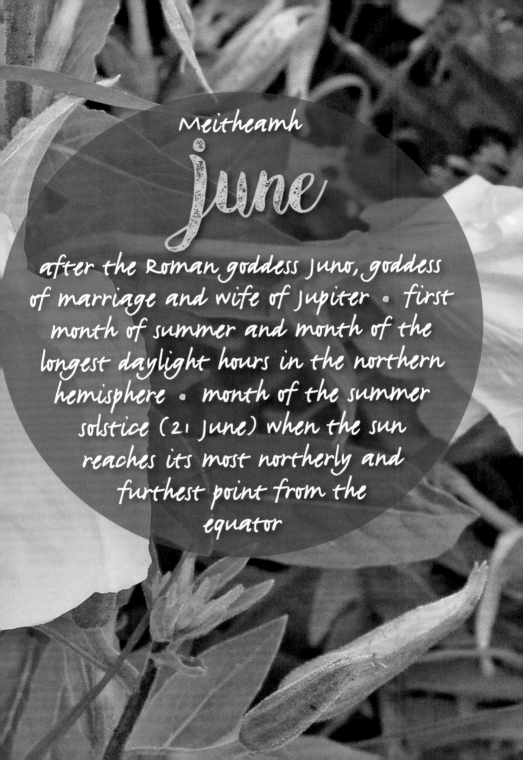

Meitheamh

june

after the Roman goddess juno, goddess of marriage and wife of jupiter • first month of summer and month of the longest daylight hours in the northern hemisphere • month of the summer solstice (21 june) when the sun reaches its most northerly and furthest point from the equator

MANY YEARS AGO, in the era of the film camera, I was guilty of sounding the death knell for a plant. All I did was stop to photograph it.

It was on Lamb's Head in County Kerry and it was the first time I had ever seen a **Large-flowered Evening-primrose**. I only took a few frames as the light was fading, but as I captured the image, a car passed by slowly. It was getting late so we decided to come back the following day when the light might be better. You can probably guess what happened when we returned – the lovely Evening-primrose was gone. It posed danger to neither man nor beast, but I can only suppose somebody took it for his or her garden. I suspect that it was whoever had driven by while I was taking the photo the previous evening. As a result I am now extremely careful of drawing attention to any plant and have been known to get up very early in the morning to try to capture an image before there are too many people around. And for those tempted to try it, it's not really worth digging up wildflowers and hoping they'll survive the trip home. They tend to wilt quite quickly and more often than not they won't like the conditions in their new home and will just fade away and die. So perhaps it's best to leave them where they are.

Large-flowered Evening-primrose |
Oenothera glazioviana | Coinneal oíche mhór

WE FOUND 'OUR' BOAT, tied up beside the quay along with several other fishing trawlers. Climbing on board, we seated ourselves on the wooden seats beside the gunwale. And we waited. After a while, more holiday-makers joined us, taking their seats wherever they could find them. We idly wondered when the trip would begin.

It was June, sometime in the late 1970s. We were spending two weeks in a cottage at Crohy Head, near Dungloe in County Donegal, with our two children and their friends. The weather was absolutely woeful but it never dampened the pure pleasure of being there. We enjoyed some superb walks, particularly in the evenings when the rain seemed to go and water a different parish. There was one direction we always preferred, along a narrow road that closely hugged the coastline. Tall, rough sea stacks stood a short distance offshore. In a previous life they must have been part of the exposed granite cliffs, but now stood separate, nature's evolving

Greater Butterfly-orchid

sculptures. It was a good place to watch Choughs, shiny black crows with red legs and long, curved red bills. They tumbled and wheeled overhead – sometimes we counted up to two dozen at a time – thrilling us with their acrobatic aerial displays, talking to one another in their unique, secret language – '*tscheeeaah –tscheeeaah*'.

Some time during our first week, Pete and I had agreed we'd take the youngsters to Arranmore Island as soon as the weather became a little more settled. I had my own, not-very-well-hidden agenda – a search for **Butterfly-orchids**, hitherto unseen by me. In Ireland, we have two native Butterfly-orchid species, Greater and Lesser. Both similar at a glance, there

Lesser Butterfly-orchid

are quite a few subtle differences, but of course it is difficult to compare two species if you only have one on hand to examine. Briefly, both bear loose spikes of greenish-cream flowers. The main differences are the lip and the pollinia – the pollen masses at the end of an orchid's stamens. The pollinia in Lesser are parallel, whereas in Greater they converge above in an inverted 'V'. In Lesser Butterfly-orchid, the lip is short (6–10mm), whereas in Greater Butterfly-orchid, it is longer (10–15mm). Also, Lesser Butterfly-orchid is less green than Greater Butterfly-orchid. I had heard that one of these species grew on the island – I didn't know which, but would be happy to find either. It fell in nicely with a trip to an island, a real treat for all of us.

Lying 5 kilometres off the Donegal coast, Arranmore is our second largest island after Inis Mór, one of Galway's Aran islands. With a population in excess of 500, the mainstay of the island's economy is tourism and its Gaeltacht status is a major attraction for language students in summer. Our son, Nik, and our daughter, Petra, were excited at the suggestion, as were their two pals, Owen and Edwina. So, on a bright sunny day, midway through our second week, we made the trip.

In more recent times, access to the island is by two ferry services from the fishing village of Burtonport – one conventional and one fast. However, at the time of our visit, local fishing boats served to transport tourists and other passengers. This form of travel was to prove an enormously enjoyable part of the day.

It was no great hardship sitting at the quayside, waiting. As the boat rose and fell, its blue, plastic fenders rubbed against the wharf, squealing and squeaking as they were squashed between wood and stone. We listened to the wheeling and squawking of the pearly-white gulls and idly watched the comings and goings of fishermen and tourists. The boat began to fill up, some holidaymakers, some locals. A couple came on board. She was tottering in high heels and wore an extremely tight red skirt, both of which somewhat hampered her efforts to board the boat elegantly. He was almost completely hidden behind an enviable range of expensive camera

Curlews in flight

equipment. In a North American accent, he asked the man who seemed to be in charge, 'When does the boat get going?' to which the response was 'When she's full.'

There was some stifling of mirth from the other passengers, eyes meeting in complicit amusement at the look of incomprehension on the visitor's face. And we waited. After some more time had elapsed, another man, who looked like he could be the skipper — he was wearing a navy cap — came on board. He sized up the payload and gave the nod to the first man, who passed around taking the fares. The loud thump of the engine told us that we might 'get going' soon. A couple on bicycles were the last people to join us and then we were off.

The trip probably took thirty to forty minutes; it was many years ago and I can't be sure. But one thing is crystal clear: my recollection of the way that the craft was handled as it left the port and headed out towards Arranmore. This journey must call for precise navigation skills. The passage out into the open sea is through a relatively narrow channel known as Rutland Sound. This is a strait separating Inishcoo and the Rutland islands. Its surface is a mass of swirling eddies.

Some forty years earlier, in 1935, a major tragedy occurred when nineteen of Arranmore's young people were drowned in these treacherous waters. Most of them were 'Tattie Howkers' or harvesters, young men and women who had been working at potato gathering in Scotland. Their seasonal work was over and they were returning to the island with their hard-earned money, but their yawl hit a submerged rock a short distance from the island. The sails were pulled down swiftly but the boat overturned

and all on board were swept into the sea. One family lost eight members. There was only one survivor of the tragedy.

We arrived safely that day and, for a while, Pete and I walked inland on tracks leading to higher ground overlooking the island and the ocean. The views back to the Donegal coast were magnificent. I found not one single Butterfly-orchid – Lesser or Greater – in spite of hunting over quite a wide area, but I forgave the island for not giving up all of its secrets. The 'nature bit' had not transferred down the generation at that stage so Nik and his pal Owen amused themselves by playing the game machines in a small entertainment arcade near the harbour. What they probably remember most about that day was hitting the jackpot and more than quadrupling their holiday pocket money. Petra and Edwina sized up the local 'talent'.

As we left the little port that evening, we saw another similar-sized trawler, which seemed to be taking the same route as we were. We had a feeling that there might have been just a little bit of competition to see which craft would get back first. Our boat clipped along at a great rate of knots, almost skimming along the top of the shiny water, again full of curling currents. The low sun illuminated sparkling rainbows of droplets from the trawler's bow wave as the boats wended their way between the islands. Astern, the outline of the large island grew steadily smaller and as Burtonport came into view, our companion boat dropped back slightly, allowing us to reach the quayside first. It was one of those 'we all came home, tired but happy' days.

Lesser Butterfly-orchid | *Platanthera bifolia* |
    Magairlín beag an fhéileacáin

Greater Butterfly-orchid | *Platanthera chlorantha* |
    Magairlín mór an fhéileacáin

They say that every cloud has a silver lining … I found that to be true once.

I had enjoyed being a canoeist for many years, being the bow paddle in a Canadian canoe that Pete skippered from the stern seat. We'd had great little meanderings along various waterways with Nik and Petra – as children – seated amidships and we loved the facility it gave us to observe wildlife, particularly birds, by getting close to them without their realisation that we were 'human'. But I had come to the stage in my life where getting down into a small craft was just too difficult. A dodgy hip had caused some problems so canoeing and I had to part company. Over the years, spare-part surgery had been taken on board by both of us – carefully timed to take place during winter months so as to avoid missing the best part of nature's year. These events proved very successful but even so, on one particular holiday in County Kerry in 2008, I knew I would have to bow out and it was with great reluctance that I waved off the next generation – and Pete – down the River Sneem, towards the sea.

Feeling sorry for myself, I grouchily wandered, camera in hand, onto a large patch of sandy waste ground close to the estuary. Then the clouds parted and I saw it – **Blue-eyed Grass** – one of the most striking flowers imaginable! It had small clusters of flowers that were open to the sunshine, each with five blue petals surrounding a golden centre. It was my first time to see this rare species, which has only been known in Ireland since the middle of the nineteenth century, in just a few western locations. However,

Sneem, County Kerry

as a wildflower photographer I had sought it out before, without success, and so it seemed to me all my birthdays had come together that day. It felt like one of the seven dwarves had morphed into another – Grumpy became Happy!

Blue-eyed Grass | *Sisyrinchium bermudiana* | Feilistrín gorm

Blue-eyed
Grass

Glenveagh, County Donegal

THEY WERE IN my eyes, in my hair, inside and behind my ears, eating away at any bit of exposed flesh; in fact, they were just about everywhere, even in places where I didn't know I had places.

It was a June day and I was in gorgeous Glenveagh, in the heart of the Derryveagh Mountains. The previous day I had been asked to take a few people on a walk to help them identify some of the wildflowers growing in that beautiful Donegal valley. The event went well and there was a good turnout of adults and several small children who were fascinated when they were introduced to another world – the world they could examine through a hand lens. We were lucky that the threatened thundery downpours stayed away.

But what I really wanted to do was to go further along the shore of Lough Veagh, to see if I could find **Lesser Twayblade**, a small member of the orchid family I had never seen. I knew its preferred home was among moss-covered deciduous trees, and that these little wildflowers were known to inhabit one or two such locations in the valley. It was a warm, humid sort of day; ominous rumbles and creaks bounced around a heavy, cloud-laden sky. I walked for an hour or so and then I spotted a mossy, wet place among woodland trees – their ideal habitat. I looked very carefully to see if I could spot any of these little plants. Oh yes! They were there, all right, way down in a mossy dip between the trunks of two trees. It had to be them. I climbed down into the little dell and realised that the light there was very bad. It would be extremely difficult to get a good image of these little plants but I would give it my best; they deserved it. Lesser Twayblades are really quite small, only reaching about 20 centimetres high. Each one has a loose spike of 2–3mm reddish-green flowers and a pair of shiny heart-shaped leaves, hence 'Twayblade' – two leaves.

Lesser
Twayblade

129

That was when the fight began: in the red corner, the midges – in the blue corner, me. My goodness, was it difficult? No, it was impossible. I was doing my damnedest to set the camera for the best possible outcome, but as for trying to hold it steady – not a hope. I was being eaten alive. How could such a minuscule creature cause so much torment? If you squeeze one between your forefinger and thumb, it disappears, leaving only a dampish smudge – and yet they can bite and bite and bite. I have read – somewhere – that there are twenty-nine different species of these tiny terrorists in Ireland. I also know that they serve a useful purpose within the natural world, such as providing food for swallows, frogs, bats and carnivorous plants like Sundews and Butterworts. But why can't those hungry little females look for their protein somewhere other than the human body, particularly mine? I believe that it is only when they are pregnant that they bite, to satisfy the nutritional needs of their developing eggs. However, my love of Mother Nature's insects deserted me that day and I make no apologies for having caused a manic mass extinction.

Because the available light was poor, I was forced to use a very slow shutter speed. This allows as much light as possible into the lens for each exposure, adapting to the prevailing conditions for the best outcome. It also meant I needed to hold the camera really steady if I wanted to get a reasonably sharp image. Normally this is not a problem – I rarely use a tripod for flower photography, depending on relatively steady hands – but this was different. I was getting hotter and my temper was becoming shorter. It was just as well those little children on yesterday's walk weren't around. That strange old lady was now using the sort of flowery language not found in any nature books.

I could only flail about with my hat, trying to swipe the little demons but to no avail. In the end, I snatched a few pictures and got out of that midge-laden sauna, breaking into the nearest thing to a run that I could manage. My long-held love of animals had finally failed the test.

Lesser Twayblade | *Listera cordata* | Dédhuilleog bheag

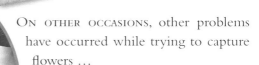

Spring Gentian

ON OTHER OCCASIONS, other problems have occurred while trying to capture flowers ...

Much, much earlier, while still in the age of the film camera, I knelt down on the stony shale of the Burren with my friend Anne. We weren't praying but doing our best to get photographs of **Spring Gentians** in a high wind. With stunning blue flowers, each on its own stem, they stand erect in the short grassland. They were the last stragglers, probably having been at their best a few weeks earlier; how many times have I heard 'You should have been here last week – they were just superb'? I decided that I would use my last remaining film of thirty-six frames and would devote the entire film to getting the best possible images of this species. Hunching over the camera to prevent any light from ruining a new, unexposed film, I loaded up and closed the camera. It was to be an enormous effort to produce at least one good photograph of this Burren species, one for which the word 'iconic' is frequently used. Anne spread her anorak wide, making a buffer

Drystone wall in the Burren

against the wind, protecting and sheltering the little flowers as much as possible. The shutter clicked over and over as I changed settings and angles, looking for the best picture possible. The window in the camera told me that the thirty-six exposures were taken. In those days you couldn't review your images at the back of the camera and there would be a week's wait for the film to be processed before I would know if they were any good.

When I got back home to Dublin, I opened the camera back very carefully and my spirits hit the floor. The little perforations along the side of the film had never engaged with the sprockets that turned the film along, from frame to frame. The film had therefore not been exposed at all – no photographs had been taken!

Spring Gentian | *Gentiana verna* |
Ceadharlach Bealtaine

DIFFERENT HABITATS can cause different problems. Thinking back to that time in Tacumshin, I still get a sinking feeling.

Tacumshin Lake, County Wexford, is a Special Area of Conservation. A lagoon that lies in the south-east corner of Ireland, it is separated from the Celtic Sea by a ridge of sand, pebbles and grit. It is a brackish body of water, home to a diverse range of waterfowl, such as the winter-visiting Greenland White-fronted Geese, Whooper and Bewick's Swans.

A few summers ago, we spent some time there, watching three Marsh Harriers – one male and two females – displaying their stunning aerial acrobatics as they drifted over the reed beds in search of food, such as frogs, fish or small birds. The vegetation around the lake included low-growing species like **Lesser Sea-spurrey** and **Sea Aster**, but on this particular visit, I was looking for a **Northern Marsh-orchid**. This native Orchid bears a spike of rich, deep-purple flowers, each with a diamond-shaped lip covered

Sea Aster

Lesser
sea-spurrey

133

with an arrangement of lines, loops, curlicues and smudges. Above the lip are more petals forming a little hood and this protects the inner, reproductive parts of the orchid. Long spotted leaves surround the base of the plant. Wet ground such as machair and damp meadows are its preferred habitat. Perhaps it might grow close to Tacumshin, I thought, and Pete and I decided to go and have a look for it.

We approached the lake from the north and wandered slowly along a rough track between areas of reeds and low-growing willows, the pathway deteriorating on occasion into very soggy puddles and pools. A couple of times, as we stopped to look at some bright turquoise dragonflies, we felt ourselves sinking into the soft ground. Where there was a break in the reeds, the sodden grass yielded a few Spotted-orchids, but no Marsh-orchids. Eventually, the saturated ground was becoming less and less firm beneath our feet and, realising we couldn't progress any further, we decided it was time to turn back. That's when one of my wellies got utterly stuck, jammed fast in the mud. I had hit a particularly soft spot and both of my feet had sunk to at least eight inches below the surface of the pathway.

I had one trek pole with me which I leaned on and my left boot freed up a bit but then the right one sank lower, almost up to the lip around the top of the boot. Pete was behind me — he hadn't got to this particular bit of ground yet — and he passed me his trek pole. I struggled and struggled but the right boot stayed put and although I managed to move my foot up, towards the rim, I couldn't extricate the boot; in fact it had now sunk

Northern Marsh-orchid

further and had almost disappeared into the quagmire. The boot was gripped tightly by the pale brown mud, which made disgustingly squelchy noises every time I tried to get it out. Pete had now started to laugh. Of course it was a cue to call me a right stick in the mud. His mood was contagious. Amid fits of the most infantile giggles, we heaved and hauled, while I tried to balance on one foot, leaning heavily on the trek poles, trying to introduce a little stability into the situation. But the more we tried to get the boot out of the mud, the more it stayed put. It was all quite Laurel and Hardy. I turned and tried to pull the boot out of the ground but then my left foot started to sink.

After some minutes of trying to get myself and my boots out of this mucky mess, I caught sight of a large bird, flying towards us and into the reedbed, close by. It was a Cuckoo. Perhaps it was looking for the nest of a Reed Warbler, one of the poor unfortunate bird species that unknowingly play foster mother to this bird's chick. The Cuckoo lays one egg in the nest, among the host's smaller eggs. The Cuckoo chick hatches first and then he or she heaves out the other eggs, one by one, using its back to lift them up and over the rim of the nest. Left as the sole infant in the nest, it gets fed by the foster parents who don't notice this is not one of their own, even when it passes them out in size. Before very long, it is fully fledged and ready to take its first flight to the African continent, where it overwinters.

The Cuckoo finally settled on a post close to the path, its wings drooping, its tail raised, in a completely typical pose. Such a handsome creature, its slate grey head and shoulders giving way to horizontal stripes across its lower breast and underparts. It was the best sighting of this bird I had ever had. It stayed in position, still as a statue – like the plastic herons in suburban gardens – challenging me. I knew I couldn't get to my camera, which was in my backpack, and my own position was anything but stable.

At this stage I decided it was time to cut my losses and, yielding my wellie to the soil, I staggered slowly out of the mire. Although on a very uneven keel, I managed to fish out the camera but, of course, in doing so

I disturbed the perfect pose of the Cuckoo and away it flew, mocking me with its call — 'cuck-oo cuck-oo'.

I limped back to the car, one foot booted, one foot wet and bootless. When I got home, I chopped the top off the single boot and it now serves as an unusual flowerpot — one with a story attached.

And a footnote — I subsequently found that gorgeous Marsh-orchid in a relatively dry area of Ballyteigue Burrow, also in County Wexford. Perhaps, a lesson had been learned — when nature takes hold, it is best just to look around you and appreciate the moment.

Lesser Sea-spurrey | *Spergularia marina* | Cabróis mhara bheag
Sea Aster | *Aster tripolium* | Luibh bhléine
Northern Marsh-orchid | *Dactylorhiza purpurella* |
   Magairlín corcra

THE DAY I found a **Kerry Lily** is still remembered vividly by Nik and Petra. They tell me that they were commanded to get down and have a really close look at this little beauty because they might never, ever, see one again. They were somewhat unimpressed but they tell me that, to this day, they remember dropping to their knees and gazing at the plant in dumb obedience. They even recall its silvery-white colour.

This was in the early 1970s. We were in Derrynane in County Kerry and taking a walk across Abbey Island, a piece of land that is only ever cut off when a very high tide occurs. I had been studying wildflowers for many years and had a good idea of what I had found. My excitement was mighty. I was without a camera but promised myself I would return some day with one. Fast forward a mere thirty years …

Petra and her husband, Mike, joined Pete and me for a week in Sneem, not far from Derrynane. I mentioned, quite casually, that I wouldn't mind having a little hunt for the Kerry Lily. There might even be a small prize for whoever found it. They took the bait.

Kerry Lily

We spent a bit of time poring over images of the wildflower species in various books, trying to get mental pictures of what we were looking for, then we split into two pairs and headed off over the island. Within five minutes my mobile phone displayed a photograph of the white, six-petalled flower. Petra and Mike had found them and directed us to the spot where they were plentiful. They had won the prize – no washing-up for them for the rest of the week.

The Kerry Lily has to be seen to be believed – it is dazzling and gorgeous. It has silvery-white, sparkling petals surrounding fuzzy, hairy stamens, which are crowned by golden anthers. It is one of our Lusitanian species (see page 266) and a rare, protected 'Kingdom County' jewel, found nowhere else in these isles. In 2005, when roadworks were being carried out close to another County Kerry spot where it grew, the decision was made to halt the works temporarily while two-metre screens were constructed to protect the plant from road spray and any other disturbances. Let's hear it for Kerry County Council: such a great example of a commitment to cherish one of our precious species.

Kerry Lily | *Simethis mattiazzii* | Lile Fhíonáin

Oxeye Daisy

HAVE YOU EVER heard the call of the Corncrake? It's a sound I shall never forget and one I long to hear again.

It was in a tent, pitched right beside the golden beach at Rossadillisk in County Galway's Cleggan Bay where I got to know the sound of the Corncrake as it called from the nearby meadow in the 1970s. Its hiding place, untouched by progress, was full of flowers – **Yellow-rattle** (see page 224), **Common Poppies** and **Oxeye Daisies** grew in abundance and the call of the bird, echoing its scientific name, *Crex crex*, was music to our ears, well into the night. Like us, the Corncrakes were summer visitors but their journey was from faraway Africa where they spend the winter. Pete and I filled many daylight hours gazing into that meadow, hoping to catch a glimpse of this shy, secretive bird. It is the males that do the calling, and how they teased and tantalised us, the sound being the only clue to their whereabouts. Tormented and tortured, we would try to gauge where they were from the call – one minute to the left, another it seemed, to the right – but neither of us ever caught sight of this rare bird. I have read that they are brown with a streaked crown and bright chestnut wings, facts that I can neither confirm nor dispute. Their flight is said to be 'weak and floppy' and yet they manage to accomplish an incredible long-haul journey, winging their way over more than 12,000 kilometres.

In the years that followed our stay in Rossadillisk, the number of Corncrakes fell into a serious decline and the species became threatened

Common Poppy

Yellow iris

with global extinction. When meadows were cut by hand, this little bird was safe enough, but with the advent of mechanised mowing, its status became threatened. In certain areas, grants are paid to farmers to delay the cutting of hay or silage until August or early September. By this time, most Corncrakes will have hatched two broods and the chicks should be large enough to escape the sharp blades of progress. Farmers must also agree to mow the meadows in more bird-friendly ways such as cutting it from the centre out. This enables the birds to escape without breaking the cover of the long grass. Providing patches of **Common Nettle** and **Yellow Iris** – both of which can grow quite tall – is also encouraged, as other early vegetation is usually too low-growing to give enough shelter to these amazing creatures.

We were possibly among the last to hear the Corncrake's call in that area in the late 1970s. For many years after that, Skylarks and other birds continued to sing high above the hay meadows, but down among the summer vegetation the sound of the Corncrake was no longer heard.

Local people remember that when the birds came calling again in 2014 it was a cause for much rejoicing, the sad silence having been accepted as the end of a particular soundtrack to so many rural lives. Perhaps, they say, the birds have now come back to the vicinity because sites where they were relatively undisturbed on Inishbofin and Turbot Islands are getting crowded. Good news all round. Also, their numbers are increasing in parts of Mayo, such as the Mullet Peninsula, and some of the islands off Donegal. This may tend to offset the destruction of their nests in the Shannon Callows, which have been subjected to summer flooding and where they no longer breed.

I returned to Rossadillisk in 2016, hoping that perhaps I might again hear the call of this bird. I didn't. It would have been such a lovely resonance of our past and, I hope, their future.

I walked down to where the lovely sandy beach had been and was stunned to see what nature had done in the intervening years. No longer was there a strand of fine golden sand. Great rocks and stones had been

Rossadillisk in 1973 (left) and 2016

hurled onto the coastline by the sea and it was difficult to reconcile my memory of the past landscape with what I was seeing.

Incidentally, much earlier in the last century, Rossadillisk – from '*ross*' (meaning promontory) of the '*duileasc*' (meaning dulse, a type of seaweed) – was once a village, home to more than the Corncrake. Cleggan Bay is remembered by most people as the arm of the Atlantic where the devastating Cleggan Disaster occurred. One October night in 1927, along the western seaboard, forty-five fishermen were drowned during a major storm that arose whilst they were mackerel fishing in the bay. This had a devastating effect on the local communities. Of those who perished, sixteen came from the village of Rossadillisk, which became derelict in a matter of a few years.

Common Poppy | *Papaver rhoeas* | **Cailleach dhearg**

Oxeye Daisy | *Leucanthemum vulgare* | **Nóinín mór**

Yellow Iris | *Iris pseudacorus* | **Feileastram**

ALTHOUGH IT IS an extremely attractive-looking plant, the next time you see it in bloom, please chop off its flowers. Honestly, I mean it seriously.

The first time I saw its unusual pink flowers, it was growing on the banks of a small river in County Donegal. It was 1980, the place was Crolly, and when I eventually identified it, I found that it was quite new to Ireland. And it was very handsome. Each large pink flower appeared to have an upper helmet-like section and there were two lower petals meeting to form a lip below. Insects were buzzing away inside the flowers, deep in the spurs at the rear. The flowers were suspended by threadlike stems from the top of their 'helmets', connecting them to larger stalks. The plants were tall, some reaching up to 1.5 metres. They had hollow, brownish-red stems, long pointed leaves and they swayed elegantly in the breeze.

Some time later I was in a garden centre in Dublin when I saw the very same species for sale. On its label, as well as its Latin name, was the name by which it would become commonly known and ultimately loathed – **Himalayan Balsam**. In the years since I first saw it, it has flourished and spread – mainly down rivers where its seeds float, allowing it to proliferate further downstream every year. These days it is high on the list of invasive aliens as it thrives in our warm climate and finds plenty of nutrition in our soils, unlike those of its original homeland where it has to face a cold climate and impoverished soil, conditions which keep it in check. Sadly, it shades out many of our native species, particularly along watercourses, and as it is an annual plant, when the plant has finished its role of setting seed, it dies away.

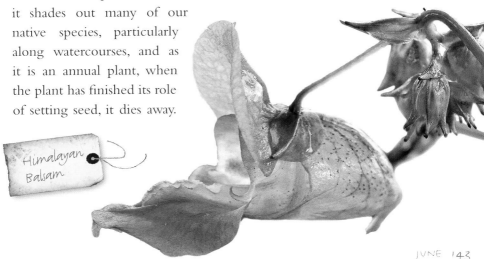

Himalayan Balsam

This in turn causes erosion of our riverbanks. It is also well designed to spread its seeds. The long, club-shaped pods have an ingenious mechanism: when they are touched, they explode, hurling around 800 seeds from each pod for at least 7 metres. Even a stiff change of wind can cause this to happen. So, while it is undeniably a good-looking species, please destroy it whenever you get the chance.

Himalayan or Indian Balsam | *Impatiens glandulifera* | Lus na pléisce

ANOTHER OF NATURE'S unwelcome introductions paid us a visit last year. It was a sobering encounter.

I was helping Pete to clear out our pond, which, as a result of our overenthusiastic planting programme, had become overpopulated. The plants needed to be culled and we set about the difficult work of 'pruning the pond'. It was a sunny autumn day and we were well prepared for the job with all the necessary gardening tools, plastic sacks, wellies and even a wetsuit, which Pete had to don in order to get down to the roots of some Water-lilies. 'Health and Safety' also insisted he wear a flotation device as the bottom of the pond was incredibly slippery and I didn't want a drowned corpse on my hands. While we were heaving and hauling on the surprisingly tough, heavy rhizomes of the Water-lilies, I spotted a teeny little flower growing at the edge of the pond. I contained my impatience for as long as was necessary and then, when we broke for lunch, I got down on the ground and tried to have a closer look at it without falling headfirst into the pond. I didn't want to pick it in case it was that wonderfully elusive, rare species, which all botanists aspire to find and have named after themselves. I could just imagine it … a two-word scientific name with the second word being '*devlinii*'.

I got out the books, the hand lens and measuring tape and went about the business of 'keying it out' – a process of elimination which should,

New Zealand Pigmyweed

in theory, lead to an identification. It worked, and the day suddenly became overcast and sad. This little plant turned out to be **New Zealand Pigmyweed** or Australian Swamp Stonecrop. All the way from Down Under, it is classed here as a High Impact invasive species. It has tiny whitish-pink flowers, each like a four-pointed star. It is a relatively recent arrival (first recorded in the mid-1980s) and its sale in garden centres is now banned. It has spread throughout the UK by the discarding of waste from aquatic garden features, and it carpets ponds, canals and lakes with dense blankets of fleshy vegetation. So far, it has been found at only a few locations in Ireland, but it is extremely difficult to eradicate, reproducing

Marsh-
marigold

from the tiniest of fragments. I probably introduced it, unknowingly, with some **Marsh-marigolds** I got from a friend. She had been unaware of this interloper's existence, until she looked closely at the margins of her own pond. I tried to scrape every last trace of it from our pond in the autumn when I first found it, but it romped back, hale and hearty, to greet me the following spring. The outlook is gloomy.

It is a sad fact that a good number of the places I visited some decades ago have declined. No longer are they able to provide a home to many of the species recorded there in the past. Invasive alien plants are ethnically cleansing some habitats and changing the environment for much of our wildlife. Habitat destruction is also resulting from changing farming practices, pollution, wetland reclamation and climate change. Learning about the relationship between wildflowers and other species that come under the umbrella of 'wildlife' in Ireland has led me to understand how fragile all of our ecosystems are, and how much we depend on each component of our natural environment.

New Zealand Pigmyweed | *Crassula helmsii* | Crasal Nua-Shéalannach

Marsh-marigold | *Caltha palustris* | Lus buí Bealtaine

AN INTERESTING part of the Burren and a favourite walk of mine is along an uphill track which leads from the ruins of Formoyle church, close to the bridge over the Caher River, and up onto the shoulder of Sliabh Eilbhe.

At any time of the year this is a lovely way to spend a few hours, but it is especially rewarding when the **Fragrant-orchids** are in bloom. Scattered along the sides of the track, they stand about 25 centimetres high, bearing spikes of scented, pinky-mauve flowers with long, downward-pointing spurs. On one occasion, Pete and I were walking up this track when we became aware of a strange singing sound. It was eerie and we couldn't tell precisely what or who was causing it. We hoped it wasn't someone in distress. We stopped, cupping our

Fragrant Orchid

Limestone landscape

hands to our ears to try to work out where it was coming from. The tone would rise a note or two, then go back down to where it had been. It was somewhat unnerving, almost ghostlike, and we couldn't fathom it out. It got louder and more sinister as we rose up the hillside. And then we came around a bend in the track. There it was – a rural quintet of wind instruments in the shape of a five-barred metal gate, complete with holes through which the wind was, literally, whistling. We played a tune on it, blocking several holes with our fingers, in random order, enjoying the novelty of it and relieved that it wasn't the sound of someone in trouble. The Burren can be full of surprises.

Fragrant Orchid | *Gymnadenia conopsea* | Lus taghla

WE HAD NEVER been away anywhere without our parents and, as he drove, Dad prepared us for the experience of staying with his three genteel relatives. He told us to be sure to say 'Please' and 'Thank you', to mind our table manners, and to always be sure to use the butter knife. Alas, I had dry toast the first morning as there was no butter knife in the dish. Such a dilemma. The next morning I did as all the others did and used my own knife.

My father had quite an extended family, including, in a generation above his, three sisters: Emily, Winifred and Veronica Wynne. These ladies, who seemed to my young self to be very, very old, welcomed us – my sister Janet and me – into their home, Tigroney, in Avoca, County Wicklow, for a few weeks over three consecutive summers in the early 1950s.

When I cast my mind back to those visits, sometimes it is the sounds I remember most – sounds of the Wood Pigeons cooing on the large lawn beyond the bay window of the house; sometimes it's the damp smell of the old flagstoned kitchen; sometimes what I remember is the simple freedom of shedding my shoes and socks and running barefoot across the damp lawn. But my strongest memory is of 'Cousin Winifred', as we were taught to call this soft, kind lady. Small, with a slight stoop, she always seemed to be in good humour, open to our endless questions and somehow I felt more comfortable with her than with her two sisters. She was the middle child of three daughters and so was I. Perhaps that was why we bonded.

Each sister was different from her siblings, with the family's talents and aptitudes lying in many areas. Emily was trained in design, Winifred was a brilliant botanist and Veronica a gifted artist. In the early 1920s, Emily and Winifred returned to Avoca from London where they had worked in the censor's office during the Great War. Being excellent linguists, their job had been to read letters coming into the country – in a number of languages – and censoring those deemed to be a threat to national and military security.

Along with Veronica, they set about revitalising the 200-year-old mill that adjoined their property. Originally used for grinding wheat and corn and for weaving wool, it had provided clothes for local workers at the nearby copper mines, as well as blankets. Now it was in dire need of renovation, and the sisters, at a time of great hardship, were also seeking to create jobs. Over several decades, their sense of design and colour, together with their commercial expertise, would bring the business, Avoca Handweavers, into the global market.

Winifred's botanical and horticultural knowledge was the force behind their use of the subtle, soft colours for which they became best known. In their large, walled garden, they grew the plants she knew would provide delicate, refined dyes for the woollen mills, and she spent time experimenting with lichens, which generated many tones of green, orange, yellow and red. She used **St John's Wort** – the yellow flowers providing hues of yellow, green and maroon. From **Purple-loosestrife** came brown and purple dyes. **Bramble** produced shades of green, black, blue and yellow – depending on which part of the plant was used. I recall seeing roof-high hanks of wool drying in the big open yard at the mill, the colours of the yarns echoing those in my tin paintbox where little rectangles of burnt sienna, raw umber, ochre and sepia lay side by side. The sisters dressed in garments made from Avoca cloth – Emily wearing tones of blue, Winifred in shades of rust and brown and Veronica clothed in purples and mauves.

I still cherish pieces the sisters created in Avoca – rugs, shawls and bags, each with its subtle blend of colours, so reminiscent of the plants among which they lived.

Winifred (left) and Emily Wynne, early 1900s.

Image by kind permission of The Library of Trinity College Dublin

slender st
john's-wort

Primula 'Julius Caesar' at National
Botanic Gardens, Glasnevin

How often I have wished that I could have been there as their contemporary. I would dearly love to be able to revisit our time there and take on board the wealth of knowledge these ladies had to give. I go mining for memories now, some reluctant to be found, hidden behind seams of irrelevant trivia. However, there is one totally clear memory I have of a day when Winifred shared some of her wisdom and her philosophy with me. Remember, this was an extremely accomplished botanist and horticulturist who had bred many cultivars in her County Wicklow greenhouse, including the delightful Primula *Julius Caesar*', still surviving in a few family gardens as well as in the National Botanic Gardens in Dublin.

She began by explaining nature's evolution of plants over the millennia, from blue-green algae emerging from the oceans, right through to the buttercups in our fields. Using words I could clearly understand, she pointed out how birds and flowers were so much cleverer than we were, each knowing what it has to do to survive, to keep its head up and carry on, no matter what.

'Nature cannot be ordered,' she told me. 'It has its own way and time and finds its own place in the scheme of things.'

She brought her philosophy a step further, using the weaver's craft as an analogy for her beliefs.

'Our life's journey is the warp – the lengthwise thread in weaving – and what happens to us, what influences us, is the weft – the yarn which crosses the warp. The warp is a strong, tough, durable fibre, the weft can be any size, any colour – it can change as it weaves its way across; it doesn't even need to match what went before it or what will follow, it will just be part of the cloth which represents a life.'

As we walked along the woodland path that led from the big house to her walled garden, she pointed out some of the wildflowers. Among them

Tigroney, Avoca,
County Wicklow

Marsh Woundwort

was **Marsh Woundwort** and she stopped and picked one of the spikes of purple flowers, showing me how each of the flowers had tiny guiding lines to help bees and other insects in search of nectar.

Cousin Winifred told me that this plant was named Woundwort: 'wound' as it was well known to have healing properties and 'wort' from an Old English word for herb or plant – '*wyrt*'. It had been used widely, along with various mosses, to dress thousands of wounds in the Great War and it was used to staunch the flow of blood as well as being an antiseptic. Sadly, Charles Wyndham Wynne, the youngest of her two brothers had, in June 1917, died of wounds in Saint Omer while serving as a captain with the Royal Garrison Artillery. He was twenty-two years old.

I recently returned to Tigroney, which was on the market. It must have been over sixty years since I had been there, but the memories came flooding back. The house was in poor form, the walled garden completely overgrown. I wrote to another cousin who had also stayed there as a child and I told her about its condition. She sent me a lovely, positive reply, saying, 'One day, the right person will come along and turn it around because they will be the one with the vision.'

Vision was what those three sisters had and I am so glad they shared it with us.

Slender St John's-wort | *Hypericum pulchrum* | Beathnua baineann

Purple-loosestrife | *Lythrum salicaria* | Créachtach

Marsh Woundwort | *Stachys palustris* | Cabhsadán

Seen on the wing in June

The **Wall Brown**, true to its name, basks in the sunshine on old walls. Its eggs are laid on grasses such as Yorkshire Fog and Cock's-foot. It is seen here on Bramble.

The **Silver-washed Fritillary** is found mainly in the south but is now spreading northward in wooded areas. It is the largest of our fritillaries, with silvery underwing. Seen here on Purple Toadflax. Eggs are laid singly on Dog-violets.

The **Ringlet** flies in late June and July in meadows and hedgerows. It has velvety, white-fringed, chocolate-coloured wings, with rings on the hindwings. Larval foodplants are grasses.

The **Comma** was first recorded in 2000 in Ireland and has been migrating here ever since. It is seen mainly in the south-east and has even begun to breed there in small numbers. Flies in woodland and gardens. It lays its eggs on the Common Nettle. The adult is seen here seeking nectar from a Buddleja.

Left: Comma
Below: Wall Brown

Left: Silver-washed Fritillary
Below: Ringlet

Montbretia

Iúil

july

after Julius Caesar —
the month of his birth

J ULY, THE SEVENTH MONTH OF THE YEAR, is usually the hottest and the month in which the greatest number of wildflower species are to be seen in Ireland. Some of these will have started to bloom earlier and are now beginning to go to seed, whereas others are only emerging, opening up in the balmy warmth. Long, sultry days begin to shorten, ever so slightly, and in the countryside, warm nights carry the unmistakeable sounds of summer.

*sunset near Ballitore,
County Kildare*

IT WAS GETTING late in the day. We needed something to eat and a place to lay our heads for the night and then we saw the signpost. It pointed to Dursey Island. The minute I saw it I knew that something had been set in motion and there was no going back. I had always wanted to visit Dursey Island (*Oileán Baoi* – island of the bull, in Viking Norse) and there it was, just a few miles further down the road. The die was cast.

It was a warm, windy week in July, some time in the late 1990s, and Petra and I were spending some mother-and-daughter time together. Petra had lived for some years away from Ireland and it was such a treat to have her company again. We had travelled from Cork city to Glengarriff, along the southern part of the Beara Peninsula and past Adrigole.

For those not familiar with this part of Ireland, Dursey Island lies across a reef-strewn, narrow stretch of water, a short distance from the tip of the Beara Peninsula in the south-west. Rugged, awe-inspiring, astounding, magnificent, breathtaking, tremendous: there are not enough adjectives to describe this part of the world. I knew of Dursey Island and its unique claim to fame – it is connected to the rest of the country by Ireland's one and only cable car. I had long wanted to travel across the sound to the island, probably as much to experience the terrifying thrill of the short trip, hanging high in a metal box over the churning waters, as actually being on the island.

We stopped close to the end of the peninsula and were lucky enough to find that the bed-and-breakfast close by had space for us. Warmth and hospitality were in abundance, the welcome given to us was second to none and a very pleasant evening was spent listening to the history, stories and legends of Dursey Island and its people. Our appetites were whetted and we decided to pay the island a visit the next day.

Perhaps I am being more than a little economical with the truth. 'We' didn't decide to visit the island. I hang my head and admit that I wanted to visit the island so much that Petra hadn't the heart to do other than agree to the plan. I have a feeling that she was terrified by the thought of the cable-car crossing, but because she is a kind, gentle person, she indulged me, never once mentioning that she had developed vertigo in her time away from home.

Absorbing and mulling over what we had been hearing about the island, we retired to bed. Next morning we set off for Dursey Sound, just a small distance up the road. The cable car station stood stark and skeletal against the pale silver clouds and the steely sea. The small box, in which we would place our trust, our lives and our hopes for deliverance, swayed in the wind. After the business end of the transaction was complete, we stepped into this frail bundle of engineering expertise and looked at each other with very

Petra prepares to board Dursey's cable car

serious, nay grave, expressions. The door closed and we held hands. I would have been a little happier had I not seen a square of cardboard pinned to the inside of the box which read 'Abandon all hope, ye who enter here.' Perhaps Dante had crossed the inferno known as Dursey Sound before us? On the opposite side of the little car was another message – it was Psalm 69: 'Save me, O God; for the waters are come in unto my soul. I sink in deep mire, where there is no standing: I am come into deep waters, where the floods overflow me.' Someone with a dark sense of humour had left this jovial legacy. Another suggested that at least one cow had been a previous passenger.

And then … we were off. Suddenly hanging about 250 metres above the sea, neither of us could resist the temptation to look down. Black rocks thrust up their knife-edges above the five-fathoms-deep frothing tide, taunting us. The car swung to and fro in the wind, terrifyingly. It must have been about ten minutes of suspension – in so many ways – before it came to rest just above the grassy landing spot. We stepped onto the island, the wind eating our words out of the air, and we gathered ourselves together again, slightly stunned.

The island is a little over 6 kilometres long and 2 kilometres wide, and only reaches 252 metres in height. There weren't too many cable cars listed for trips back later in the day and we didn't want to spend the night on the island so we decided to start walking and see how far we could get before it would be time to head back.

Inhabited now by only around a half-dozen, Dursey Island's population increases with summer residents who visit the island and stay in a few of the previously abandoned homes, now restored. The 1841 Census of Population recorded 358 persons living on Dursey and those islanders didn't suffer as badly as others during the Famine. By harvesting shellfish and seaweed, many of them managed to hang on to life, but by 1851, only a mere ten years after that census, the population had dropped by over 100 to 249, some areas faring better than others. However, it wasn't just the Famine that caused the drop in numbers – evictions also contributed to the decline. One century later, the 1951 census recorded ninety-six people living on the island and this dropped forty-five years later to a mere nine.

On the day that Petra and I walked across the island, we didn't meet a soul. The only inhabitants seemed to be grazing sheep and the graceful swallows, swooping in and out of a derelict house, flapping their wings against the dusty windows before finding their way out again. There was an eerie feeling, seeing so many abandoned buildings that once rang with the sounds of family life. The views were stunning – we could make out the Bull, the Cow and the Calf, rocky islands that hung on the dark horizon, as well as the unmistakeable outline of the Skelligs.

The vegetation was low-growing, as one would expect in such a windswept habitat. There was one particular shrub that seemed familiar until I got close to it. It looked like Gorse, the shrub that can light up the Wicklow Mountains, even in winter. On closer examination, these golden flowers were a little smaller, the colour of the spines seemed to be greener, and they were not as deeply furrowed as the Gorse in County Wicklow. And the strong coconut scent was missing. I took some photographs and wondered if this was a different species, filing it away in the back of my mind for another day.

Petra and I walked almost the length of the island but, being a little anxious to get back before dark, we retraced our steps briskly and the cable car lifted us back to the mainland. It was quite an experience and one I should love to repeat. I should add a little note here: this cable car, the lifeblood of the island, has been in operation since 1969, before which cattle used to swim across the sound on their way to market, beside and behind their accompanying flotilla of boats. That cable car was since replaced around 2009 and, for health and safety reasons, the new system does not allow adult cattle to travel in the cable car, only permitting a limited number of smaller animals such as sheep or calves. It must be a tough life, living in such a small community. There are no shops or schools and to endure the rigours of the Atlantic gales, the isolation and the lack of what most of us take for granted, surely takes a very special temperament.

Western Gorse

It was to be almost twenty years before I saw that species of Gorse again and this time, in County Mayo, I was able to identify it. It was **Western Gorse** and I found it growing close to the Great Western Greenway, the 44-kilometre track

taking walkers and cyclists from Westport to Achill. Western Gorse is a low-growing shrub compared to the more common Gorse and it only flowers from July to September, unlike its cousin, which blooms all year round, with a particular peak flowering time in April. That day, in Mayo, I also encountered for the first time a large colony of a native fern that has survived, almost unchanged, for over 100 million years, the imposing **Royal Fern**.

Royal Fern

Western Gorse | *Ulex galii* | Aiteann gaelach

Royal Fern | *Osmunda regalis* | Raithneach ríúil

GROWING UP in Dublin in the 1940s and '50s, we were lucky enough to spend a couple of weeks each year in Derrynane, County Kerry. In our first holiday, long before the days of campsites or mobile homes, we camped just above the beach with an uninterrupted view across to Lamb's Head. In subsequent years, my parents rented a converted boathouse for a fortnight each summer and with the accommodation came a little rowing boat. It was all pure bliss, but nothing was as exciting as visiting one of the islands.

There was Lamb Island, which lay across the mouth of Derrynane Bay, and Abbey Island, an island only at a very high tide. Abbey Island was wild and untamed, with massive clefts and chasms, deeply cut into the dark rock of the island, the sea churning and foaming way below. I used to terrify myself thinking of what would happen if I fell into one of these crevasses – it was the stuff of nightmares. We would walk with our parents up onto the island, often spending the day circling this magnificent piece of land or sitting gazing at the waves, beyond the Thrift-covered rocks. Two well-known wildflowers

Thrift

crowded together in the abundant grassland, **Purple-loosestrife**, with its tall spikes of ragged magenta flowers, and the bright orange flowers and long, pale-green leaves of **Montbretia**, an introduced species but now 'more Irish than the Irish themselves'. Larks sang overhead.

There was a little cemetery on the island, not far from the beach. On one occasion we saw a funeral party make its way across the sand, the coffin borne on the shoulders of eight of the mourners as the bereaved threaded their way along a pebble-strewn track. It seemed a dreadfully lonely place to leave someone, I thought at the time. Now, more than half a century later, I think it must be so peaceful there, with only the wind and the birds for company.

Purple-loosestrife | *Lythrum salicaria* | Créachtach

Montbretia | *Crocosmia x crocosmiiflora* | Feileastram dearg

Purple-loosestrife

Creeping
Yellow-cress

OUR PARENTS ALWAYS told us we were never to stare. 'Having a gawk' was discouraged. Now I sometimes think that if all curiosity is blunted, life becomes a lot duller. It occurs to me that often, by watching someone for just a little bit longer than you feel is permissible, you allow the person being watched to indulge in a form of performance. There's a sort of unwritten contract that says 'You watch and I'll carry out this little bit of street theatre.'

Whenever I think of **Creeping Yellow-cress**, I call to mind a delightful cameo, a little incident that happened a few years ago. It was on the day I found that species. My first encounter with a particular wildflower is often irrevocably etched into my memory and this one is no exception. However, the memory of that particular day is of more than that plant. It was a lovely low-key happening I fondly recall.

It was a July day in 2010, one of those sultry dog days at the height of summer. Pete and I were visiting a favourite spot, Inistioge, on the banks of the River Nore, in County Kilkenny. The road through this gem of a village crosses the river by way of an eighteenth-century ten-arched bridge. Close by are the 200-year-old Woodstock estate, the remains of a thirteenth-century Augustinian Priory and the twelfth-century Church of St Mary.

Creeping-jenny

Banded Demoiselle

A short way upstream from the village is a remarkable marshy meadow where I had found several plant species earlier that year. I was interested to see how the wetter parts were progressing as the hot July days took their toll on the surrounding vegetation. There was still a substantial area of the field that was swampy and in it I found a large colony of **Creeping-jenny**, an evergreen species with pretty golden flowers. Some of the plants were completely submerged so that many of their flowers seemed to be drowning. In another area there was a great stand of **Yellow Iris**, with incredibly beautiful **Banded Demoiselle** dragonflies darting around them in the sunshine.

We spent some time savouring the peace of the meadow and then made our way downriver, stopping a short distance below the village at a quay where the river level was low for several feet out from the bank. It was a spot where we often interrupted our wanderings long enough to enjoy a bit of lunch. I walked towards the river and looked over the quayside and saw a little yellow flower poking its head up. I knew I'd never seen it before and so I searched for some way of getting down to have a better look. At the same time, Pete had strolled further along the lane and came

River Nore at Inistioge, County Kilkenny

quickly back. It seemed he had found it, too, and his was much easier to access. I always get such a great leap of excitement when I see something new to me – if not to science – and this was no exception. Out came the books, the hand lens, tape measure and camera and the identification process began. It turned out to be Creeping Yellow-cress, a small member of the Cabbage or Brassica family and not a very common species. After a while, my heart rate returned to normal and I took my photographs for future reference.

We got our lunch out and sat down on a picnic bench, thoughtfully located on the quayside. The sun was shining, the river sparkled and a thousand insects flitted and skimmed across the surface of the water. The only sound was the gentle lap of the river as it meandered across the gravelly shallows. On the far bank, a great forest of trees rose high into the sky, deciduous and coniferous close together, all stretching up to the light.

Sandwiches almost eaten, flask almost empty, we were about to pack up and leave when a large blue van arrived, drawing a horsebox behind it. Both of us were curious and it seemed that unanimously we decided to be plain, old-fashioned nosy and stay a little longer.

What looked like an extended family alighted from the van and two of them, lads in their early twenties perhaps, went around to the back of the horsebox. They undid the latch and, using a halter, led out a large piebald mare. She was a beauty. We couldn't resist admiring her and complimenting the lads on their lovely animal. They didn't mind in the slightest and seemed immensely proud of the superb creature. We returned to the picnic table and sat back down to see what would happen next.

After about ten minutes, the horse was led slowly down the little boat slip bordering the quay and across the shallows at the edge of the river. The lad who was leading the horse had removed his shirt and was now naked to the waist, just wearing jeans and brown leather cowboy boots. He led the animal across the gravel bank and towards the deeper part of the river. We expected him to stop there and let the animal drink but they both went on, carefully picking their way into the deeper water. The horse was clearly quite used to immersion in the cool slow-flowing river. They both walked on until the lad was up to his waist in the water. At this stage he put a hand into one of the back pockets of his jeans and took out a tall, white, flattish container. We recognised it as a bottle of shampoo, which bore the brand of a well-known cosmetic company.

The boy reached up, inverted the bottle, and squeezed the thick, white shampoo along the creature's back, across her shoulders and into her long, dark mane. Putting the bottle back into his pocket, he stretched up and massaged the shampoo through the horse's coat until her body was covered in white foam. When he had that task completed, he started to scoop up the river water in his two hands, splashing it all over the animal, the sun catching the sparkling drops and creating little rainbows. The mare clearly loved it, as she stood, just twitching her flanks and swaying her head from side to side while he worked away, rinsing the shampoo from her coat. When every single trace of the foam had gone, he turned towards the quay and led her back gently to the waiting family. By now, quite an audience had gathered to witness the spectacle.

As he got to the shallow gravel bank one of his family tossed a towel down to him and he began to rub her coat. When he deemed her to be dry, he flung the towel back up. We were sorry to see the spectacle come to an end, but it hadn't quite. In the style of a circus ringmaster, the lad, who I suspect was enjoying his audience, threw out his arms and, in a loud and perfectly clear voice said these never-to-be-forgotten words: 'Because she's worth it.'

Creeping Yellow-cress | *Rorippa sylvestris* | Biolar buí reatha

Creeping Jenny | *Lysimachia nummularia* | Lus an dá phingin

THERE WAS ALWAYS an air of fun in the back of Dad's car when we knew we were going to Glenmalure. We loved the trip itself but the best bit was when we would arrive at the top of the valley and he would turn the car towards the river.

With great anticipation and delight we would thrill as the car slowed down and crossed the Avonbeg River by the Barravore ford. We were allowed to wind down the back windows of the car and gaze into the running water below. What excitement – driving through a river! This was a crossing made by stonemasons whose craftsmanship and skill I only came to appreciate when I was an adult, realising what a work of art they

Part of the ford at Glenmalure, County Wicklow

had created. When the flow of the river was reduced in summertime, you could see, in the clear shallows, that the flat slabs lay next to one another, across the riverbed, just like a modern-day paved patio. It was a monument to workmanship of the highest order.

We were on our way to see my father's cousin, Kathleen Lynn, in the County Wicklow cottage where she spent her weekends, away from the city she worked in all week. The house was just a couple of hundred yards up the track from that ford and she always gave us such a lovely warm welcome. With her special encouraging way, she would draw us out, initially with a few questions about ourselves until she got us talking, and then she would engage us in conversation. Perhaps it was her work as a paediatrician that gave her this extraordinary talent. It was small wonder we loved going to visit her.

Kathleen Lynn.

Image by kind permission of the Royal College of Physicians of Ireland, catalogue number SU/8/3/18.

Kathleen Lynn was a feminist, socialist, nationalist, and paediatrician and co-founder of St Ultan's Children's Hospital in Dublin. I consider myself so lucky that our paths crossed. She was the person responsible for giving an enormous boost to my early interest in wildflowers by showing me, through a large magnifying glass, the intricacies within a wildflower.

She was an extraordinary woman with many talents but what I loved about her was the sparkle in her eyes and most of all, her slightly mischievous smile. She wore a little 'pince-nez', a nineteenth-century style of small, round spectacles which sat on her nose, without the support of side ear-pieces. One end of a narrow gold chain was attached to the pince-nez, the other being pinned to Dr Lynn's collar or to a hairpin. She wore her hair, as did many older women of the time, in a long plait, twined around her head. She had a lively, round face with rosy cheeks but it was her eyes that held me always. Our lives overlapped by only thirteen years, but this small lady left such a deep impression on me that it seems our connection lasted much longer.

She was born near Killala, County Mayo, in 1874, a second daughter to Reverend Robert Lynn, the son of a doctor, and Catherine Wynne, a clergyman's daughter from Drumcliff, County Sligo. In her early years, although not experiencing it herself, she saw the great poverty, deprivation and hardship that was being suffered. In a stable and privileged position at the end of the nineteenth century, she was given an education. This was initially at home with a governess and continued at Alexandra College in Dublin and then in the UK and Germany. She studied medicine at the Catholic University Medical School and became the first female doctor to obtain a residency at the Royal Victoria Eye & Ear Hospital in Dublin. Her career progressed through several other Dublin hospitals until 1919, when she and her great friend, Madeleine ffrench-Mullen, established St Ultan's Hospital for Infants at Charlemont Street in Dublin.

In the aftermath of the Great War, conditions in Dublin for a large number of families were extremely bad. Poverty-related diseases, inadequate housing and nutritional deprivation were all-pervasive. The incidence of venereal disease increased with the return of men from the battlefields of Europe. This contributed to infant mortality and to deaths of mothers in childbirth. The outlook was bleak. The all-female staff at St Ultan's had an enormous task before them in trying to improve the lives of those who crossed their threshold. But they succeeded and I have personally come across people who came into contact with Dr Lynn and who, like me, greatly benefited from her help, in one way or another.

By introducing me, through a hand lens, to the intricacies of an orchid species, Kathleen Lynn gave me a wonderful gift. On one of our family visits, we went for a wander up the Glenmalure Valley. She took me by the hand and led me towards a low-growing **Heath Spotted-orchid** that grew some distance up a path known to Wicklow hillwalkers as Table Track.

Heath
spotted-orchid

Crouching low, she drew her magnifying glass from the pocket in her tweed skirt and held it between me and the plant. I think they would call that 'a defining moment' in today's parlance. I was well and truly hooked!

So many changes have happened during the years since those visits to Glenmalure. One of them involved the very ford we crossed over all those years ago. Some decades after Dr Lynn's death in 1955, the ford was changed utterly. It was originally laid down at the beginning of the nineteenth century to give the British military access to higher ground in the Wicklow Mountains. They were seeking to flush out insurgents, scattered throughout the valley and still at large after the 1798 Rebellion. This military force was stationed at Drumgoff Barracks, close to the intersection between the Laragh/Aughavannagh road and the road to Greenane. The barracks is now in ruins, its only visitors being Sand Martins that nest in the nearby sandbanks each year.

The Barravore ford remained intact for almost two centuries but during the recession of the 1980s it was rebuilt and, as a result, the original exquisitely crafted ford was obliterated under a mixture of concrete and plastic piping. Only a few remember what lies beneath this new creation. However, it is not only the artefacts of the built environment that have suffered. As certain aspects of our daily life develop and progress is made towards improving the living conditions of our growing population, other elements alter, often in unforeseen ways. The environment has suffered from the results of land drainage, peat extraction, changing farming practices and many other activities — all aimed at improving our lives in different ways. Certain levels of society have also been damaged through the lack of sufficient attention from those charged with a duty of care. By her courage, energy and resolution and in her challenges to the authorities of her day, Kathleen Lynn set a unique standard.

Heath Spotted-orchid | *Dactylorhiza maculata* | Na circíní

WE SAT AROUND a large table – walnut, I would say. Shining cutlery, gleaming glassware, crisp white linen napkins, a floral arrangement at the centre, red roses, white carnations. There were eight of us and in front of each was a large circular plate, covered with an ornate silver dome, a leaping dolphin at its top. Four waiters stood, evenly spaced, around the table and, at some signal – unseen by us – each of them picked up a dome in either hand with a practised flourish, revealing a small, artistically arranged dinner. The performance was replicated at several other tables throughout the lavishly decorated and furnished dining room. Not the company canteen but an extremely exclusive country hotel in County Limerick, renowned for its cuisine, its golf course and conference centre. My friends envied me. If only they knew.

A two-day conference of European Heads of IT was taking place and I was deeply involved. Apart from coordinating all sorts of different aspects of this meeting, I had the job of organising the programme for the 'trailing spouses'. This term applied to the wives – all the Heads were male – who needed to be kept entertained while their husbands were doing the important work of the day. Poor helpless creatures in a foreign country, they needed to be looked after in order to keep the corporate boat on an even keel. It also gave me the chance to show off some of Ireland's treasures and I'd arranged a couple of day trips to my favourite places, the first one being the Burren.

The next day started very, very early, so early it was almost the night before. One of the trailing spouses phoned me at 5.30 a.m. to tell me she had no ironing board. Even in my sleepy state, my heart bled for her. A delegate rang to say he couldn't lock the safe in his room. We had an unexpected duo of vegans and a coeliac who hadn't alerted us prior to coming. The photocopier was on the blink, the overhead projector was overheating and so were quite a few of the attendees. The hotel staff were utterly professional so, having ironed out as many problems as I could, I swallowed a quick cup of tea and headed out to where the female 'league of nations' was assembling.

Léim an Phúca Beag and Léim an Phúca Mór, Turloughmore Mountain, County Clare

'It's a bit misty in Galway Bay,' Tony told me as he shepherded the ladies into his large shiny coach. 'Let's hope it lifts a bit, they're saying it will later on. Fingers crossed.' Tony was solid, totally reliable and his sunny disposition meant he was always cheerful.

The ladies seemed to be in an optimistic mood. Some wanted to look at craft shops, two wanted to place bets on a race at Epsom, others had questions for me about Ireland. For most, it was their first time here and I was keen for them to go home with good memories. As we headed north, I could see what Tony meant. The mist was more like fog. We stopped in Ennis where our punters placed their bets, then onto our first scheduled stop, the Cliffs of Moher. I had spent some time telling the group about the majesty and magnificence of this amazing feature of County Clare's west coast but the fog was right down. There was no possibility of seeing the superb cliffs. A coffee break had been arranged there, but it hadn't taken account of a burst water main. No coffee, and worse still, no water in the Ladies' loos. It was getting a little embarrassing, but Tony found us a lovely hostelry near Fanore where the plumbing was in working order. We had coffees there and the group dynamics started to kick in.

Lunch had been booked in a nearby hotel and along with the meal, a glass or so of wine. The food was good, the service excellent and we raised glasses to the gaiety of nations. The day was looking better outside too. It was time to move on.

As we were making our way slowly through the lobby, towards the hotel door, one of the trailing spouses suddenly collapsed. She seemed to subside slowly, landing softly with a certain elegance on the deeply carpeted floor and – thank God for small mercies – into the recovery position. Although I was a trained first-aider, getting a body into this arrangement isn't always easy. I might have broken her arm or leg if I'd had to try, especially under the close scrutiny of the audience gathered around us. She was out cold.

A staff member suggested that he call a local doctor while I, taking out my brick-sized mobile phone, rang our hotel. I needed to inform the woman's husband and to see if there was anything he knew that might help. Meanwhile, two of the women were scrabbling furiously through the collapsed lady's handbag to see if they could find a clue to the reason for her sudden fall. Great excuse for a 'nosy', too, I thought.

It took a while for the husband to get to the phone and, selecting my words carefully, I began to tell him what had happened to his wife. As I talked to him the doctor arrived. The husband refused to discuss the problem with me, saying instead, 'Put me onto the doctor', which I did. Most of the ladies had gone out into the sunshine. I hovered in the lobby. When the doctor finished the call, he handed me back my phone, saying, ever so quietly, 'I'm afraid that this lady is an alcoholic and she's on a treatment to help towards her recovery, but unfortunately it means that if she takes a glass of wine, she will certainly have a bad reaction.'

As my eyes widened, he continued. 'I will now give her an injection and she should be fine in a few minutes, but no more alcohol for her, please.'

Just as he had predicted, within a few minutes her consciousness returned, shortly followed by her composure. We joined the group outside. She hardly spoke a word as she got on board, just 'Yes, I'm fine, thank you,' to those who enquired. The sun had burned off the fog as we motored towards one of the most scenic parts of the County Clare landscape. We were heading up the flank of Slieve Carron, the limestone pavement glowing with reflected light. As we got to the high spot of the hillside, the recovering lady made it known that she felt sick and needed to get out of the bus. Tony pulled into a parking spot and she and I left the bus. She sat on a rock, facing away from the bus, and asked me to leave her alone. It was then that I realised I had not been for a comfort stop for most of the day.

My need became quite urgent. There are very few trees in this part of the Burren to hide behind or convenient hedges to hop over but I'd been to this spot before and I knew there was one small grove of Hazel just over the brow of the hill. As quickly as I could, I legged it and, as I did what nature demanded, I spotted something growing out of a crack in a slab of limestone beside me. It had to be a **Fly Orchid**. I nearly fell over as I tidied myself up and stooped to see it more closely. Quite a rarity, this little orchid was one I had looked for so many times, without success, and here it was, minding its own business as I was tending to mine. A slender plant, it bore an erect spike of flowers in a loose spiral, the strange red-brown arrangement of petals resembling a large fly. Like the Bee Orchid (see page 83) this species mimics insects in order to

Fly Orchid

attract visitors for pollination purposes. It is a most unusual and scarce plant and I was so thrilled to have found it. It was tempting to stay there, examining its extraordinary intricacies, but as I knew I was prolonging my visit to the area after the conference, I told the plant to keep safe. I would be back. On the way back to the hotel, we picked up over £100 in winnings in Ennis. The loot would be spent in the bar that evening, the day's events not detering anyone from bending an elbow.

When we finally got to the hotel, the lady with the problem was met by her delegate husband who whisked her off quickly, without a word. They checked out before any of us knew it, early the next morning. After the conference, nature called once more. This time the call was to return to the Hazel grove and spend some quality time with my Fly Orchid.

Fly Orchid | *Ophrys insectifera* | Magairlín na gcuileanna

IT WAS A MOST remarkable bathroom. An enormous cast-iron bath stood on four curving feet, against a wooden-panelled wall at one end of the large room. Above it was a framed embroidered panel, worked in cross-stitch, which read 'A Contented Mind is a Blessing Kind'. A tall, white-framed window looked out onto the sloping garden, heavy full-length lace curtains modestly screening the occupant from a fleeting glimpse by anyone working in or admiring the garden. At the other end of the room stood what we would have called 'the toilet'. Thoughtfully located beside it was a bookcase, at precisely the right distance for those wishing to ruminate quietly for any length of time. It contained a comprehensive collection of books. Aptly enough, one of them was *Thoughts from the Quiet Corner* by the American poet Patience Strong.

It was the home of Gladys Wynne, a water-colourist of note. She painted her environment – in particular landscapes of County Wicklow – with a delicate sensitivity. An early member of the Watercolour Society of Ireland,

Auntie Gladys at her easel (above) and
(right) at her front door

her work is still very highly regarded and in many collections. She was the
daughter of an archdeacon and along with her sisters, Cerise and Florence,
was educated at home by a governess. She went on to study art and some
of her earlier paintings reflect her time spent in Italy and Switzerland, in
the company of other Irish artists. Her brother, Llewy, was my grandfather.
I never knew him but was so fortunate to have had Gladys in my life, our
lives overlapping by more than two decades.

If I had known the expression then, I would have
said she wore her talent lightly. To me she was a sunny,
cheerful person who loved us all equally, giving us her
critical but always kind assessment of the 'artworks' we
regularly took to her for appraisal. Gladys also loved
her garden but told me once that what she liked best
was finding plants she hadn't put there, but
which had arrived, unbidden, flowers
which, she said, others might call weeds.
It was she who first showed me one of
her favourites, **Germander Speedwell**, surely the
most appealing of our native Speedwell species.
This is a delightful wildflower found in hedgerows
and woodland, with the typical flower shape of
that genus – an arrangement of four petals – the

Germander
Speedwell

lower being smaller than the other three, and at the centre, two prominent white stamens. She loved it for the deep blue of its flowers, each with a small white 'eye' at its centre. Her garden birds were important to her too and she shared her stories about some of them, painting word pictures for us. The most frequent visitor to her back door was an extremely tame Robin, which she fed regularly.

We would often visit her at her home – Lake Cottage – in Glendalough. It overlooked the lower lake and behind it rose a steeply sloping garden with access to the hillside above. She always welcomed us warmly, a heavenly smell of freshly baked scones greeting us on arrival. Dressed in her floral-printed wrap-around pinny, her shining white hair smoothed across her head under a fine hairnet, she would go about the kitchen, preparing afternoon tea, warbling in a high hymn-singing voice as she worked. The song I associate her with most is one I suspect has not been heard for a long time, part of which went – 'On the road to Mandalay, where the flying fishes play'. It painted such an exotic picture in my mind. When she knew we were coming to visit, she would hide wrapped sweets among the bushes and plants in the garden and it was our great delight to run around, seeking them out.

In the entrance hall, Auntie Gladys had carefully recorded the height of each member of the family who ever visited her. Along the side of the door that led into her living room was a panel with pencilled horizontal lines, each one leading to a name and a date. She drew a new line for each of us every year, usually around our birthdays. With the help of a ruler – which she placed on our heads – she would mark the wall where the ruler touched it, creating the new record. We often wondered which of us would grow to be the tallest. Would any of us ever reach the height of the previous generation whose records were still visible on the panel? Would we even pass them out? Any time she had the hall painted, she made sure that the panel was left untouched. It was very precious to her.

A vase full of **Bog Cotton** (as Common Cottongrass is colloquially known) stood on one of the wide windowsills of her living room. Typical

Bog
Cotton

of heathy acid land, wherever this sedge grows its soft white tassels speckle a mossy backdrop of bogland. The flowers are greeny-brown, small and slight, each becoming a tiny seed, attached to a pappus or feathery plume that enables it to be carried off with the wind. Clustered together at the top of narrow, erect stems, these soft tufts made a lovely display beside the window, their seed heads backlit from the light outdoors. Perhaps she picked them when she brought her easel and paints to one of her beloved spots in the valley, to work on a watercolour.

She was an avid letter writer and this windowsill was where she prepared her letters for posting. A small scales stood there, complete with a conical pile of shiny, round brass weights. When her envelopes were ready for collection by the postman – one of those unsung heroes of rural life – she would ensure that they all had the correct postage. For this purpose, she kept sheets of stamps of various values close to the scales. Around the edge of each sheet of stamps was a perforated strip and it seems she had stored away every single strip. After her death in 1968, we found that affixed to the back of each of her possessions was a square of this stamp paper. On each piece she had written, in her lovely generous round handwriting, the name of the person to whom she wished to bequeath the object. It was such a simple way of ensuring we received what she wanted us to have, without any fuss and so much reflected her gentle, kind nature.

I inherited some lovely treasures from Auntie Gladys, my most cherished being *The Birds of Ireland* (Ussher and Warren, 1900) complete with pencilled notes and records dating back to 1911. In it, she had written: *Zoë. Keepsake from Aunt G.*

Germander Speedwell | *Veronica chamaedrys* | Lus cré talún

Common Cottongrass | *Eriophorum angustifolium* | Ceannbhán

WHEN MY NINE-TO-FIVE working life came to an end, I brought into focus my lifelong relationship with nature. It was our daughter, Petra, who suggested that I share my wildflower photographs and plant information in the form of a website. I had joined the Wexford Naturalists' Field Club and with the great help of one of its members, Jimmy Goodwin, I set up www.wildflowersofireland.net. This was to prove most effective as a channel of communication with many other like-minded individuals. Both the Field Club and the website have become forums for sharing and learning about many aspects of the natural world and have enriched my life to a major extent.

My first sight of a Bee Orchid (see page 83) was when Club member and friend Janet Whelehan asked me would I like to see one. 'Yes, please,' was my unsurprising answer. She took us to Kilmichael Point, near Arklow, and showed us this amazing little species growing on the sandy cliffs. What also remains in my memory of that day is coming across **Hound's-tongue**. This is a downy, greyish-green plant with deep maroon, funnel-shaped flowers held in drooping clusters. Quite a rarity in Ireland, it was introduced from Europe into North America where it is now considered a noxious weed. And here it was, classed as rare in Ireland. One man's meat …

Janet's first passion is birds and she is quite an authority on the subject, having participated in ringing, recording and studying them for many decades. She is also extremely interested and knowledgeable on insects and particularly bees, so it seemed fitting that she took us to see our first Bee Orchid. She also showed me a Grayling butterfly (see page 241) at

Hound's-tongue

Irish
Lady's-tresses

Ballyteigue,
County Wexford,
on a day when I
found her a **Lesser Centaury**, that
tiny protected wildflower species
that bears bright pink, five-petalled
flowers.

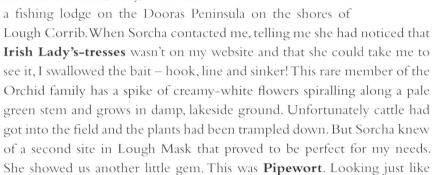

Then there is Sorcha Peirce
and her husband, Roy, who run
a fishing lodge on the Dooras Peninsula on the shores of
Lough Corrib. When Sorcha contacted me, telling me she had noticed that
Irish Lady's-tresses wasn't on my website and that she could take me to
see it, I swallowed the bait – hook, line and sinker! This rare member of the
Orchid family has a spike of creamy-white flowers spiralling along a pale
green stem and grows in damp, lakeside ground. Unfortunately cattle had
got into the field and the plants had been trampled down. But Sorcha knew
of a second site in Lough Mask that proved to be perfect for my needs.
She showed us another little gem. This was **Pipewort**. Looking just like

small knitting needles poking up through the lake's water, the domed, button-like flowerheads are pale grey. This species is only found in bog pools, shallow, peaty water and lakes. We have returned to Dooras since and found other treasures but it is Sorcha's kindness that is stored away in the part of my mind where other comfortable memories live.

I've also been lucky in meeting other naturalists, literally 'in the field'. Most of us tend to identify one another easily by our garb, principally the faded Christmas-tree look. This is caused by wearing khaki- or brown-coloured garments and draping ourselves with binoculars, cameras, backpacks, lenses and other characteristic paraphernalia.

One day, in 2011, Pete and I were walking in Newcastle, County Wicklow, as always on the lookout for the ever-changing rewards nature presents. A young man came along the path, in the familiar gear and we exchanged the usual greetings on the lines of 'Did you see anything new today? What butterflies are flying, and how about the birds?' We swapped noteworthy items of news such as the arrival, from warmer parts, of the Hummingbird Hawk-moth, a day-flying migrant to our shores. The young man was Sam Connolly – www.gardenofireland.com – and I asked him if he had ever seen **Sea-kale**, a rare native plant species that had been last sighted somewhere along the south-east coast. He wasn't sure, but would check his photographs. Then, in 2012, he got in touch, sending me precise details as to where the plant was growing. He had even chalked a small

white arrow on a rock pointing to several Sea-kale plants. A coastal species, it is a bit like a great big cabbage, with broad, succulent leaves and large clusters of white flowers. To me this was like receiving a map to buried treasure.

And then there is Jackie O'Connell who brought Paul Green and me to a soggy spot in the Dublin mountains and showed us **Bog Orchids** (see page 267). We almost got stuck in the immensely marshy ground, typical habitat for the species, but it was well worth the struggle to free ourselves. Along with so much of his experience and knowledge, taking us to see this little species was a very generous gift to both of us from Jackie.

There are many others. All of these people share a love of nature, are not competitive and unstintingly impart their knowledge with others, both amateur and professional. It certainly keeps my world turning.

Hound's-tongue | *Cynoglossum officinale* | Teanga chon

Irish Lady's-tresses | *Spiranthes romanzoffiana* |
  Cúilín gaelach

Pipewort | *Eriocaulon aquaticum* | Píbín uisce

Lesser Centaury | *Centaurium pulchellum* | Dréimire beag

Sea-kale | *Crambe maritima* | Praiseach thrá

sea-kale

The **Dark-green Fritillary** is mainly found in coastal areas and the Burren. Its larval foodplant is Violets and it is seen here on Lesser Hawkbit. Pearlescent spots on the underside of the hindwing differentiate this from the Silver-washed Fritillary (see page 155).

The **Essex Skipper** is a very small migrant. The grass Cock's-foot is its larval plant and the adult is seen here feeding on Bramble. Found mainly in grassland, the first Irish record of this small butterfly was in 2006 in County Wexford from local man Jimmy Goodwin, coincidentally the web designer of www.wildflowersofireland.net.

The **Meadow Brown** is a widespread species that flies in grassland and meadows. Its eggs are laid on grasses. It is seen here on Common Knapweed.

Left: Essex Skipper
Below: Meadow Brown

Dark-green Fritillary

JULY 189

Bog Pimpernel

Lúnasa

August

After Augustus
Caesar, first Emperor
of Rome • third
month of
summer

AUGUST IS THE BEST MONTH for observing the phenomenon known as shooting stars. These meteor showers occur on a few clear, warm nights in early August (usually from 9 to 14 August) lasting until early dawn. Known as the Perseids, they are caused by minute particles of debris, left behind by a comet called Swift-Tuttle, which orbits the sun once every 133 years. As our planet passes through this stream of dust and ice, the stream lights up and crashes into Earth's atmosphere to the delight of stargazers all over the country.

Lúnasa is also the name of the festival that traditionally ushered in the harvest season. An event with pagan origins, it celebrated the first of the new season's food and it corresponded to another festival on our island, the Ould Lammas Fair, which takes place at the end of August in Ballycastle, County Antrim.

WE SAT ON THE short, soft grass, gazing across a four-mile stretch of sea towards the Kerry coast and the MacGillycuddy's Reeks. The warm sun played on our shoulders, the sea breeze gently cooling. Far below in the crystal-clear water, seven seals were suspended, lazily flapping their flippers in a kind of synchronised swim in slow motion, their eyes focused on the strange beings overhead. Behind, we could hear the screams of the gulls wheeling in the salt-laden air. Where we sat, there was evidence of rabbit life, their burrows serving as breeding quarters for some of the birds. Further down the cliffside, the loud alarm call of Oystercatchers caused a flock of Common Terns to take flight. At times the breeze became stronger, the tops of the waves scooped, plumes of misty vapour lifting from their crests.

We were on Deenish Island. One of the sleeping beasts of my childhood, Deenish lies out in the Atlantic. Close behind it, rising steeply, is Scariff, with its forbidding monster's eye, in reality a distinct, enormous hole in the rocky cliffs at the northern end of the island. Together they presented an enduring image of two massive creatures, resting perhaps, close to the horizon. As I got older, I often dreamt of setting foot on one of those islands.

Homestead on Deenish Island, 1975

Pete, Nik and Petra on Deenish

In a nineteenth-century cartographer's notebook, which was prepared for the compilation of maps, Deenish was described as 'An Island … situated in the sea and near Scariff. An Island which would Rent at about £16 per annum.' In the 1852 census, three houses were home to twenty-one souls but by 1911 this had decreased to seven. Now there is nobody.

I wondered what it must have been like to live there, what difficulties and hardships were overcome or endured by the islanders. Even in the 1970s, before the explosion in the communication systems we now take for granted, we felt a deep sense of isolation on that island.

I only remember seeing one homestead that day, a sturdy two-storey house with a chimney stack at either end. Devoid of life, all that remained to give evidence of the family that once called this place home were a wooden settle, dresser, table and chairs. Outside, patches of lazy beds still showed their raised parallel banks, once home to precious potatoes, now like giant pieces of corduroy lying on the sloping ground. Close to the house was a well – the water sparkling, clear, tasting pure and fresh.

If I was asked to think of a colour that dominated that day it would be the bright yellow of **Common Ragwort**, spread across a large part of

Marsh
Pennywort

Common
Ragwort

the grassland near the house. An unloved but handsome plant with daisy-like flower heads and crinkly leaves, it filled several fields on that side of Deenish. In the shelter from the prevailing wind, it grew wherever it could manage to get a foothold. There were no farmers here to despise its toxicity. I wondered what other wildflowers were holding on to life on this windswept piece of land. In one damp runnel, I was lucky to find **Marsh Pennywort**, a plant with softly scalloped circular leaves – hence its common name – and the most minute pinky-green flowers imaginable, hidden away under the foliage. Another little gem was the delicate **Bog Pimpernel** with pink, bell-shaped flowers. It formed a mat across a wide, wet channel, rooting from nodes on its creeping stems. Clearly, the terrain favoured low-growing plants as the prevailing westerly Atlantic gales would have been tough adversaries for anything aspiring to grow more than a fingernail high. The only species that managed to raise itself higher

– to about 15 centimetres – in that particularly damp, windswept spot was **Bog Asphodel**, an extremely pretty plant, which has a spike of starry, golden flowers, often with as many as twenty flowers in the spike. With just a few scale-like stem leaves and rigid, sword-shaped leaves coming from the base, the plant is also very attractive in autumn when it turns a dark orange-brown colour. Once a widespread species, because its habitat is diminishing, it is now less frequently found.

We weren't the only summer visitors to the island. Wheatears scuttled across the grass, telltale black-and-white tails betraying their presence. The scratchy sound of two Stonechats came from the low-growing Gorse. High in the sky above, the Skylark's song was scattered by the wind as the bird made its tumbling descent towards the ground.

The force of the wind had gradually increased since we had arrived at the rock-strewn beach a few hours earlier. 'I'll be back for you around six,' the boatman had said, starting the outboard engine of his small craft.

The day had slipped by quickly; it was almost six o'clock and there was no sign of any boat. The gentle feeling of peace and tranquillity was quickly slipping away, too. Gathering up our belongings, we made our

Bog Asphodel

Deenish and Scariff Islands

way down to the beach. The waves were crashing and thumping against the rocks on either side. Pete and I were growing increasingly uncomfortable. We hadn't envisaged this as the way the day would unfold. We sat and waited, trying not to impart our anxiety to the children. After a while, Nik said he was hungry so we rooted into the bottom of our rucksack and took out a couple of squishy bananas which he and Petra ate with relish. I took them both up to the well where the novelty of scooping cupfuls of water kept them occupied for a bit. Pete took over, introducing a form of Poohsticks, where they raced pieces of sticks down a small stream behind the house. While they were playing, I watched the sea, combing the rough waves with Pete's binoculars, hoping to catch sight of our rescuers.

It must have been a couple of hours later when we heard the sound of a boat chugging towards the island. Then we saw it, a large fishing boat this time, not the same small craft as before; we guessed the weather conditions had deteriorated so much than the larger boat was deemed necessary. Two pairs of hands were being waved to us from some way off. The boat slowed down and dropped anchor some distance from the shore. One of the men climbed over the stern of the boat and into a small dinghy tied behind. He rowed towards the rocky shore, but there was no way he could get the boat in between the large boulders at the water's edge where the water was heaving. He beckoned to us to come out to the dinghy, shouting between his hands, his words lifted by the gale.

There was only one way for it so, holding on to Nik and Petra tightly, Pete and I waded out through the seaweed and rocks, lifting them high above the water and on towards the dinghy where they were pulled on board. It was absolutely terrifying, having to pass them over to these strangers, placing our children and all of our trust in their hands. They were swiftly rowed over to the fishing boat and transferred into its safety. Then we pushed out against the tide, holding our bags aloft, to where the dinghy had returned for us, and we climbed in. A few minutes later we were making large puddles on the wooden deck of the fishing boat, more than a little grateful for our rescuers' hard work. Our return trip, while exciting for our children, was one of immense relief for Pete and me.

The next few days the wind roared incessantly, the sea crashing against the beach, even in the inner harbour at Derrynane. It was to be a week before that storm blew itself out. We were extremely lucky to have returned safely and I am so grateful to the boatmen who made such an effort to look after us. I often think back to that unique day, remembering so many aspects of it – from the seals, floating in the clear blue sea below the cliffs, to the seabirds mewing and crying and the gaudily glowing golden Ragwort. But perhaps it is the homestead that left the largest impression on me. I wonder how it must have felt for those living there when they had to leave Deenish forever, when they closed the door for the last time on their lives on that little piece of land four miles out in the Atlantic.

Common Ragwort | *Senecio jacobaea* | **Buachalán buí**

Marsh Pennywort | *Hydrocotyle vulgaris* | **Lus na pingine**

Bog Pimpernel | *Anagallis tenella* | **Falcaire corraigh**

Bog Asphodel | *Narthecium ossifragum* |
   Sciollam na móna

Fossil

I've BEEN LOOKING at wildflowers for over sixty years so I should never be surprised to find the places where they once grew have altered. Sad to say, nature has been the loser in the main. Change comes in many ways. Sometimes it could be called evolution when perhaps the changing hand of nature itself deals a blow to the environment.

Shaped like a crooked finger pointing towards the village of Ballyvaughan in County Clare, *An Rinn* (the point or headland) or the Rine, is a low-lying promontory of sand, grass and rocks. Many of these rocks bear evidence of the geological history below this intriguing region of Ireland. Closely examined, they exhibit proof of the past in the form of fossils of ammonites, sea urchins, snails and other creatures that lived over 300 million years ago.

Today, rabbits and hares have free run over the grass, and the landward side of the spit gradually slopes towards an area of mudflat where seabirds feed, to some extent sheltered from the onshore breeze. Sometimes, a

Yellow-wort

couple of horses forage on the turf, cropping the grass and swishing insects away with their tails. And it was on the Rine that I first came across a remarkable little wildflower, **Yellow-wort** or, to give it its Irish name, *Dréimire buí* which translates as 'yellow ladder'. This is a small native annual that grows in bare, sandy soil, limestone grassland and dunes, so it is perfectly attuned to habitat such as the Rine. It has pretty yellow flowers, held on grey-green stems but a noteworthy aspect, from a botanical point of view, is the way the leaves are arranged. Classic examples of the botanical term 'perfoliate', the leaves are joined together from about three quarters of the way from their pointed tips and the stem travels through this wide join. 'Yellow ladder' is a perfect description as the leaves seem to form steps up the stem towards the flower at the top.

I've lost count of how many times I have walked to the end of the Rine and watched the seals lying on the offshore rocks, curling their bodies into sickle shapes, like large grey bananas, basking in the warm Atlantic breezes. The final metres of this walk were always a little difficult as the terrain was strewn with large rocks, scattered over time by passing storms. However, the winter of 2014 saw incredible gales that exerted greater force than had been experienced in living memory.

That January, Irish weather records were broken when a new maximum wave height of

The Rine in 2006 (left) and 2015

23.4 metres off the north-west coast was noted. In February, Met Éireann warned of Hurricane force 12 winds off the west coast, a strength at the top of the modern Beaufort Scale for measuring wind speed. Hurricane force at sea means enormous, completely white waves with foam and spray being whipped and driven through the air, massively reducing visibility. Wind speeds are reckoned to be higher than 64 knots (74 mph or 120 km/h). On land, the forecast can be for severe, widespread damage to structures, vegetation and unsecured objects and total devastation.

County Clare was hit by the destructive force of nature and millions of euro of damage was caused. I watched images on television of gigantic waves hitting Lahinch. A Ballyvaughan friend wrote and told me about the hundreds of tonnes of boulders, shingle and sand that were swept from the seaward to the landward side of the Rine, tearing up a lot of turf in the process. But it was not until I visited the area in May 2015 and saw for myself what had happened that I fully appreciated the devastation.

No longer could we walk to the end of the point. The ocean had hurled colossal amounts of sand, large rocks and giant clods of turf across the spit and had broken it up totally. The power of the wind, and the vast, terrifying might of the sea had wreaked havoc of immense proportions on this usually tranquil area. All I could do was feel totally overcome by the knowledge that this time it was not the hand of man that had changed the environment but the power of nature itself.

Yellow-wort | *Blackstonia perfoliata* | Dréimire buí

Hare's-foot
Clover

IN 1984, WORK TOOK place on the railway line from Dublin to Bray where the line wends its way around Killiney Bay. Major modifications were needed to facilitate the introduction of the DART – Dublin Area Rapid Transit – part of Ireland's suburban rail network designed to serve an area from Malahide, 21 kilometres north of the city, to Greystones, 30 kilometres south. These trains were to be powered by electricity, delivered by overhead cabling. To keep the public safe from the dangers of this massive source of power, the bridges over the line had to be altered. This included a footbridge, which took pedestrians from the Vico Road, above Killiney Bay, to a bathing place known as The White Rock, a small arc of sand on the northern shore of the bay.

Since 1977, when I first found it, I had been observing and recording an unusual species of wildflower growing right beside the old footbridge. This gem, commonly known as **Hare's-foot Clover**, is not a very wide-spread species in Ireland. The flowers do indeed resemble fluffy little paws, bearing conical heads of tiny dusty-pink peaflowers like small feather dusters. Confining itself principally to coastal areas, it is scattered sparsely across the southern shores of Munster and the sunny south-east, with a few sightings in Counties Wicklow and Dublin. At that time, I had never seen it anywhere else in Ireland and was quite sad when it completely vanished from its stronghold beside the railway bridge after the completion of the work. I looked for it every year from June to September, but there was no trace of it.

In the summer of 2009, Pete and I took ourselves to the North Bull Island, Dublin's best-kept secret as a location for wildflowers. We were looking for **Marsh Helleborine**, a member of the Orchid family, which bears loose spikes of small flowers. It's hard to describe these but I shall try … each flower is comprised of three purple/red sepals, narrow red-marked white upper petals and a frilled lip below. This lower lip is white, is notched and has red veins and a central platform which has a yellow crinkled splotch above the white frills. This is one occasion where a picture certainly helps!

We parked the car on a road that was covered by windblown sand, the dune-binding Marram grass waving alongside the road in the warm breeze. And then … I almost fell, trying not to step on the many, many plants of Hare's-foot Clover growing beside the long, narrow rolled leaves of the Marram grass. What a happy renewal of acquaintance that was! We found superb swathes of Marsh Helleborines too, but it was refinding an old friend in the Hare's-foot Clover that made my day.

Hare's-foot Clover | *Trifolium arvense* | Cos mhaideach

Marsh Helleborine | *Epipactis palustris* | Cuaichín corraigh

Marsh
Helleborine

St Dabeoc's Heath

As if they were towing the ferry on invisible strings, eight dolphins swam through the water a few metres in front of the craft, leaping and plunging as they went. The spray sparkled like falling diamonds, the animals' streamlined, silver-grey bodies surging upwards and forwards, briefly dropping into the sea only to rise again in a superb, continuous movement.

They led the ferry for most of the way from Tarbert, in the Kingdom County of Kerry, across the Shannon Estuary to Killimer in the Banner County of Clare. It was spectacular. We felt privileged to have seen such a magnificent display. We didn't know that there was an even better one to come.

On that trip, I was in search of a wildflower that grows only in Connacht. This was **St Dabeoc's Heath**, a species belonging to the Lusitanian Flora (see page 266). It is exceptionally handsome with loose spikes of large, bell-shaped magenta flowers, each with four lobes, which turn back slightly at the narrow outer end of the flower.

It was our first time to travel on the recently opened route and the weather gods were being kind to us. We didn't stay in the car for the twenty-minute journey but instead walked around the open deck, taking in the air and the view, seeing whatever there was to be seen. We were rewarded by the sight of those dolphins – truly, a most unexpected treat. It was thrilling and we loved it, talking about it most of the way up to Cleggan where we were staying the night.

Next morning, we headed towards the head of Cleggan Bay where we had heard there might be a good chance of finding St Dabeoc's Heath. Across the narrowing channel, the townland of Ballynew rose on the opposite side of the bay. We drove slowly, scanning the panorama before us. Then the spectacle began.

A small distance away from the shore, a sight met our eyes like nothing we'd ever seen before or since. At least fifteen Bottlenose Dolphins were dancing in the water, leaping from the surface, flipping and splashing back down, resurfacing over and over again. At this stage we were out of the car, standing and watching in total incredulity – it was a glorious bravura display.

Then, as if by silent command, the pod broke in two, each group heading away a short distance until they stopped, turning to face the other half and, swimming forwards, the two groups dovetailed into one other. As if this was not enough, one of the larger creatures rose from the surface, appearing to stand on his tail in the water, looking directly at us, and he repeated this action several times, flopping back into the shallow water. We were both certain that he was communicating with us. It was a truly phenomenal performance.

We found our plant species too, and it was a good find. There was plenty of it growing beside a small waterfall in the stream that flows into Cleggan Bay. The handsome flowers and dark-green foliage grew in profusion in the banks. It was in great order and was so satisfying to see growing in such healthy abundance. I was really pleased to have found them, but how could they possibly compete with the spectacle of our dolphins?

St Dabeoc's Heath | *Daboecia cantabrica* | Fraoch na haon choise

THE 'ADDED-VALUE' ELEMENT was also present the day we sat in the car at Bishop's Quarter in the Burren, eating our sandwiches, wishing the weather would change for the better. I was hoping for a chance to photograph some **Greater Knapweed.** This handsome plant is like a deluxe version of a thistle, not prickly but carrying quite a feathery top to its cluster of tiny florets. The purple florets emerge from an inflated, globular calyx, itself coated with a pattern of bristly brown bracts.

Greater
Knapweed

Curlew at Bishop's Quarter, Ballyvaughan, County Clare

Every now and again we turned on the wipers to clear the relentless rain off the windscreen and perhaps get a glance of one of Pete's birds. Oystercatchers and Curlews were feeding between the low rocks, and gulls were wheeling around above. The car was being buffeted by the wind, not another person was in the car park – we reckoned they all had more sense.

The flask was emptied, the bananas and biscuits eaten and we were tidying up the debris of our lunch when Pete spotted him – or maybe it was her – a small, brown creature, scampering across the rocks, running under, over and through the dark golden seaweed. We both scrabbled through the untidy car, finding our binoculars, focusing on him as he dipped and scurried back and forth across the foreshore. Trying to make a mental list of what we were looking at, we both spoke aloud: 'Brown upper fur – white bib and underneath – bits of white on ears – tip of tail seems to be black'.

No, it was definitely not a Pine Marten. Although they live in some numbers in the Burren, we knew we could recognise one on sight, but this was quite different. And no, we don't have Weasels in Ireland. Neither was it an Otter, which is a much larger creature altogether.

Perhaps we had spent too many hours during our teenage years watching *Looney Tunes* and *Merrie Melodies* in the Grafton News and Cartoon Cinema, that great institution of the 1960s, but this little fellow was more agile than any Speedy Gonzales or Wile E. Coyote. We watched him for at least ten minutes and then he ran off, out of our sight, never to be seen again, at least by us. We subsequently found out that what we had seen was an Irish Stoat, a native and protected species whose diet includes fish, which is probably why he was hunting along the shore. Unlike many other stoats, the Irish Stoat keeps his brown coat all year round – there's no need to change into a white one for camouflage in winter as we really don't have much snow. We would dearly love to catch sight of one again but although we have spent umpteen hours sitting in the same spot, we have never had such fortune again. Once more, hope springs eternal.

Greater Knapweed | *Centaurea scabiosa* | Mínscoth mhór

I CAN NEVER serenade him with 'You don't bring me flowers': it just wouldn't be true. He has brought me many (never cut flowers – perish the thought!) and in so doing, he has introduced me to several new species. Who am I talking about? Well, you've already read his name many, many times over the last few chapters so perhaps I ought to introduce you formally now: please meet Pete Devlin, my best pal ever, my soulmate.

I met Pete almost sixty years ago and after 'going together' for five years, Reader, I married him! During those six decades we have each widened our horizons, learning so much about our chosen spheres of interest within the natural world. We have made the transition together from those grey, narrow days of mid-twentieth-century Ireland. Now, in what passes for 'retirement', we are enjoying a wider focus on the more colourful, information-rich world of the twenty-first century and all it has to offer. Pete calls himself my 'roadie'. He accompanies me all over the country, 'worrying weeds' as he terms it, often in places where he might also find a bird or two. But there are times when he heads off on his own and who's to blame him? Botanical walks never made anyone fit and he claims that they are 'a good walk banjaxed', what with all the stopping and starting and looking down at what is growing beside your feet. He has brought me home some super finds – sometimes a small flower in his pocket, other times just a word picture, depending on the abundance of the species he has found.

Pete is interested in many aspects of the environment but his main focus is on birds. He likes to walk around Killiney Bay, the scene of many of his childhood holidays, mainly to watch the sea birds – hoping someday that Fulmars might return to nest on the cliffs. They've been gone a long time. After one walk, he drew me an image of flowers resembling small yellow suns on green stems. He had found them growing at what was then called 'The Vico Men's Bathing Place'. This was an area of deep water where male swimmers took to the waves – in the nude. My curiosity was aroused – only about the plant, I hasten to add – so I ventured down the slopes, eyes averted from the sea as I didn't really want to watch the locally called 'Pink Seals' cavorting in the water. The plant turned out to be exactly as he had depicted. It was **Golden-samphire**, a relatively scarce

Golden-samphire

Rock sea-lavender

perennial only found in a few coastal locations, showing yellow daisy-like heads during late summer months. Another time, he found **Rock Sea-lavender**, a pretty plant with upright spikes of small purple flowers on dry zigzagging stems. This he found growing above the high cliffs overlooking this magnificent bay. Then there was the day in 2007 when he came back from a Dún Laoghaire walk. He told me over dinner that there was a white flower growing on the West Pier he didn't think he'd ever seen before. When I went to see it the next day, I could only hazard a guess as

small
Teasel

to what it was. It was Dr Matthew Jebb, then Taxonomist at the National Botanic Gardens, who confirmed it as a newly arrived species of Teasel. At first feared it would become an invasive species, it seems to have vanished from that location since then and now the only distribution dot for the species in Ireland is for the site where Pete found it. As I write, he's out for his walk … I wonder what he'll bring home this time.

Golden-samphire | *Inula crithmoides* | **Ailleann Pheadair**

Rock Sea-lavender | *Limonium binervosum* | **Lus liath aille**

Small Teasel | *Dipsacus pilosus* | **Leadán úcaire beag**

KERRY HAS GIVEN me so much. As a youngster, I had great freedom-filled holidays there and when we had our own family, I decided it was time to introduce Pete to this wonderful place and share it with Nik and Petra, too. So, one August in the 1970s, we towed our wooden rowing boat from Dublin to Derrynane behind the old Renault 4L.

Both car and boat were packed with 'stuff' such as a large canvas tent, oars, sleeping bags, food for several armies, wellies and a Seagull outboard engine. After a slow journey we arrived at our destination as the sun was smouldering in the western sky. We stopped close to the estuary and asked a gentleman who was walking there if he knew of anywhere suitable to camp for the night. Remember, this was in the early 1970s, long before the days of organised campsites.

'You are more than welcome to camp there,' he said, pointing to a small plot of land bordered on two sides by a Privet hedge and on the other two by the sea. 'And you can leave your boat in my haggard, if you like. It'll be quite safe.' This was our introduction to Mr Murphy, a lovely person who was to welcome us for many years to come.

What bliss it was, lying in the tent in the late evening, listening to the music of the waterfowl resonating and echoing across the flat sand of the estuary. The sounds formed an unspoken bond between those who heard them and those incredible creatures. The bubbling sound of the Curlew, the Lapwing's '*peewit*' call – all were enough to soothe any inner struggle, to create the peaceful calm that only ever comes to me by being at one with nature.

Meadow-
sweet

The field was full of elegant plants that bore hazy clusters of small creamy-white flowers and had graceful, fern-like, feathery leaves. The sweet scent of the flowers was heavenly, that of the leaves was intense, rather like the smell of almonds. This was the well-named **Meadowsweet**, a plant used in former times as a strewing plant and held most sacred by the Druids. The leaves and the flowers would be scattered through a dwelling, their strong aroma masking other less-welcome smells, and the plant's salicylic acid helping to disinfect. What I remember most about that little field was the year when we shared it with dozens of Peacock butterflies. They must have found something that particularly pleased them – perhaps it was the

Privet flowers; they certainly seemed to settle on them repeatedly – and maybe they got their nectar from them because while Meadowsweet is scented, it gives no nectar whatsoever.

The boat gave us a tremendous facility for seeing life from more than one perspective. We could get really close to birds without their realising we were their perceived enemy – humans. One particular highlight was when Pete and I were pulling the boat up after one little trip along the southern side of Lamb's Head. I suddenly noticed several erect pale-green spikes standing up in the short turf. If you have never seen **Autumn Lady's-tresses**, you have missed one of the most delightful smaller members of the Orchid family. Very small green-white flowers spiral their way up an upright stem, each flower facing a different point on the compass, the lower flowers opening first so the cluster tapers towards a point at the top. Growing in coastal locations, usually facing the sun in short grass and on sandy ground, they can be difficult to spot, but once you have seen your first one, the rest will be easier to find. One of the last flowering wildflowers of the year, it is well worth waiting for.

Autumn Lady's-tresses

Meadowsweet | *Filipendula ulmaria* | Airgead luachra

Autumn Lady's-tresses | *Spiranthis spiralis* | Cúilín Muire

The **Peacock** is a most striking species with bright eyespots on both fore and hindwings. Eggs are laid in clusters under Common Nettle leaves. They fly in gardens, hedgerows and in woodland. Seen here on Hemp-agrimony, a dusty-pink native wildflower butterflies seem to love, which grows in ditches, by rivers and on coasts.

The **Painted Lady** is a migrant from North Africa that flies in gardens and woodland. Numbers fluctuate from year to year. Its foodplants are Thistle and Common Nettle and it is seen here on Hemp-agrimony.

The **Red Admiral** flies throughout Ireland in gardens, hedgerows and woodland. Its foodplant is the Common Nettle. The underside of its wings is delicately patterned. The adult is seen here also feeding on Hemp-agrimony.

The **Green-veined White** flies in meadows and woodland. Its eggs are laid on wild Mustards and Water-cress, and this adult was seen on Common Valerian.

Left: Red Admiral
Below: Green-veined White

Painted Lady

Peacock

Wall
Lettuce

Meán Fómhair

September

september was originally the
seventh of the old Roman calendar's
ten months, thus named from
Latin 'septem' meaning seven ·
this is the Irish Meteorological
Service's first month
of autumn

EPTEMBER ... the month of endings or of beginnings? When I was young, as the long, carefree school holidays would draw to a close, so grew a deep apprehension, almost a dread, of the coming academic year. Now, with those years a distant memory, September is very different. It is a time when I cherish the flowers that linger, enjoying their presence in the shortening days. I watch the Swallows too, flocking together, forming a chorus line on the wires, preparing to take flight to their winter homes, far away.

Beech tree in autumn

There is a sad but precious feeling to these days, each good one to be banked against the colder, harsher times to come. For one whose heart beats more intensely when the wildflowers are in bloom, there is a feeling of winding up or shutting down, almost as if that's it for another year. But I have to be optimistic. I tell myself that next year I shall find and refind those that escaped me this year. I remind myself that if there was no autumn, there would be no spring; if nature has done its job properly, then the annuals will have seeded themselves, the biennials will be putting their energy into either year one or two, and the perennials will be literally going to ground for several months.

SOME SMALL DISTANCE away, about twenty multicoloured feral goats were making a metallic clatter as they picked their way across the stony ground. A large goat, with attitude and horns to match – most likely the Billy-in-chief – was accompanied by a harem of Nannies. A few little kids, on the periphery of the group, were bleating vainly for attention. We had wondered about the strong, musky odour we had smelled earlier and now we knew – Billy was on a mission to reproduce. It being the rutting season when males have an irresistible urge to assert themselves, we decided to give him and his entourage a wide berth.

Eyebright

A soft, gentle breeze freshened the late summer air and an amazing view lay before us – across Galway Bay, the hazy backdrop of Connemara and the Twelve Bens; offshore lay the Aran Islands, three distinct land masses of karst limestone similar to that below our feet. Inland and to the south was the rounded top of Sliabh Eilbhe, the highest point in the area, twin walls of stone defining the ancient green roads crisscrossing the landscape.

I was in the company of our son, Nik, who had just finished a course with AnCO, the state training agency at the time. The only member of the family who had not yet been to the Burren, he had a small gap between his course and a new job and when I suggested he might like to clear his head with a weekend away, he didn't need any persuasion. On the road down, he sang along with ABBA, the Beatles and my favourites at the time, Roxy Music. It was good.

We encountered the goats the next morning as we walked up onto Gleninagh and Murroughkilly, two elevated areas in the softly terraced hills. Great limestone slabs were spread out before us, small scrubby vegetation sprouting in the grykes between them, tiny white splashes of **Eyebright** and

gentle, delicate blue **Harebells**. The spindly, angular red stems of **Wall Lettuce** carried small bright-yellow flowers, and the prickly stalks of **Carline Thistle** bore honey-coloured velvety flowers, each surrounded by a collar of spiny, pale-yellow bracts. There were still plenty of wildflowers around, some fresher than others, maybe just hanging on until the autumn gales would tear them away. The walk was enjoyable and sharing it with Nik made it extra special.

'How about a little glass of something to celebrate this wonderful day?' Nik asked as we reached Bell Harbour, close to where we were spending our second night.

I was more than ready to slake my thirst and we found ourselves a small pub close by. Created by an extension to the front of a two-storey house, it had a certain charm. On each of the small tables was a large vaseful of garden flowers, slightly taking 'the harm' out of this being a drinking establishment. Nik has always had a mischievous sense of humour and, as

Carline Thistle

Wall Lettuce

we walked into the pub, he put his arm around me and, playing to a small audience of drinkers, he said, loudly and lovingly, 'What would you like to drink, my darling?'

Immediately, all conversation stopped and a hush descended, every head turning to see what the 'darling' looked like, with her good-looking toy boy. We were the centre of attention, eyebrows and expressions conferring, on this hussy, large amounts of scorn and contempt. I made a mental note to murder my son later. Afterwards, we walked back to our base for the night, Nik singing along the way – this time it was Johnny Cash.

I always have a not-so-hidden agenda when it comes to the Burren and this trip was no exception. I wanted to get a good photograph of **Lax-flowered Sea-lavender**. It is one of the more robust early-autumn species and by far the most common of the Sea-Lavenders growing in Ireland. It has loose clusters of small, lilac-coloured flowers scattered along

Above: Sea-purslane and Lax-flowered Sea-lavender
Right: Muckinish Castle, County Clare

its upright stems. Its seed heads often stay on the plants throughout the winter, generously helping to feed hungry members of the finch family.

The musical thread of the weekend continued the next morning. As we drove to Muckinish, an area bordering the stony shallows where the Sea-lavender might be, Nik turned on the car radio, hoping to hear a news headline – he's always been a news addict. RTÉ's *Sunday Miscellany* was on air. This is a long-running programme of 'music and musings' and we

Nik in 1985

were just in time to hear the start of the second movement of Haydn's Cello Concerto No. 1 in C Major. A magnificent piece of work, it is a personal favourite. Thought to have been lost forever, it was rediscovered in 1961, just two years before Nik was born. The pure, clear, round, singing tone of the cello in the player's careful rendering of the work was the perfect partner for this moment. It couldn't get better.

The Sea-lavender and **Sea-purslane** grew in abundance on the shingle. Both tough fleshy plants, they were holding their own, withstanding the salt-laden winds, which arrive, unhindered, fresh from their Atlantic journey. Close to the shore, mustard-coloured seaweed was draped over a tall rock like a magistrate's wig on a perruquier's stand. Beside the road, Hawthorn trees, sculpted by the gales, twisted and bent like an old man's spine, gave evidence of the prevailing wind's constant pressure.

For those unfamiliar with this part of the Burren, Muckinish is at the edge of a narrow strait; across the water lie Scanlan's Island and the New Quay peninsula. Upstream is Bell Harbour and when the tide is falling, the narrowness of the passage and its lack of depth cause the water to flow very strongly from Bell Harbour towards the sea. Pete and I had seen this phenomenon before and found it intriguing, the tide racing towards the outer channel like a river, but what Nik and I were to witness was amazing.

Imagine the scene for a moment – on your left is the open sea, on your right is the waterway from Bell Harbour with the tide swiftly emptying through that channel, from right to left. Then, suddenly, the eye catches the shapes of seals – they are leaping from left to right, against the flow – breaching the surface on their way up the watercourse. Looking like dolphins, arching, splashing, sweeping and lifting themselves at times almost clear of the water's surface, this group of a dozen or so large browny-grey animals slowly gained against the ebbing tide. Perhaps it is an everyday occurrence for these creatures. But for Nik and for me, as we watched this stunning display, we felt it was so much more. It was epic, and for a short while, we were part of it.

Eyebright | *Euphrasia officinalis* | Glanrosc

Harebell | *Campanula rotundifolia* | Méaracán gorm

Wall Lettuce | *Mycelis muralis* | Leitís bhalla

Carline Thistle | *Carlina vulgaris* | Feochadán mí

Lax-flowered Sea-lavender | *Limonium humile* | Lus liath na mara

Sea-purslane | *Atriplex portulacoides* | Lus an Ghaill

MEADOWS WERE once commonplace in rural man's environment. Expanses of grassland, they supported diverse elements of biodiversity. Originally created by Iron Age man to provide hay for winter fodder, livestock were kept off this ground to allow for the vegetation's growth. Now, authentic, traditional meadows are almost entirely absent from Ireland due in some part to the use of fertilisers. So-called improved grassland has taken the space once occupied by meadowland, with very few native wildflowers daring to show their heads.

Meadows are often regarded as being romantic, dreamy places with the sound of bees buzzing and the mosaic of colours reminiscent of an Impressionist's palette. In this space, the breeze gently 'suthers' through the vegetation; small birds scuttle and hide below the grass tops. But meadows are important for many elements of our biodiversity. They have a valuable role to play in supporting insects, essential both as pollinators and as foodstuff for birds, hedgehogs, shrews and other small mammals. All these features – and more – are what I wanted to provide. This is the story of how I went about trying to get my own small patch of paradise.

It was 2013 and the project literally kicked off when I was given a large brown paper bag of **Yellow-rattle** seeds in late August. This is a semi-parasitic annual, which, by parasitising on the roots of grasses, impedes their growth, allowing other wildflowers to thrive without being crowded out. It is a most attractive, yellow-flowered plant that germinates in spring. The flowers bloom from May to July and the plants set seed in early autumn. Those flat brown seeds are in large pods that, when dry, make a rattling sound whenever they are moved or shaken. Being an annual, after it has produced these seeds it dies away, leaving gaps for the seeds of other species. I had read about the Yellow-rattle

Yellow-rattle

method of getting a meadow started and thought, why not? Let's give it a try.

When setting out to make a meadow, the first thing to realise is that it has a much better chance of working if the soil has never been fertilised. In my case, I didn't think it had been so I took a chance and got to work. I chose an area that gets the sun whenever it shines. This is what a meadow needs: lots of warmth and sunlight.

Packets of wildflower seeds

I made sure the grass on the site was extremely short and then scarified it. What a wonderful word – scarified. It means to lacerate or score it with the tines or prongs of a rake. Then I went and got my hiking boots on. This may surprise you but when you learn how I sowed the seeds, all will become clear. I chose a warm morning when the ground was damp and softish and I walked into my little area – a smallish circle with a diameter of about 12 metres – and attacked the ground with the back, rather sharp, edge of the heel of my boot. By bringing it down sharply a couple of times, I could make a little dent or notch in the soil and I wiggled the heel in the indent each time, to make it wider. Into that groove I shook a small quantity of seeds. Then, using the heel of the boot, I stamped the seeds into the earth and scuffed whatever grass there was so that it slightly covered up the worked-on area. I repeated the above set of actions for a while – it was warm work and if anyone passing by had noticed me, they would probably have had me committed. Walking around in circles, kicking the soil vigorously and repeatedly, could get you a strange name in some places. Eventually, by the end of the day, the work was done and the waiting game began. Incidentally, choosing a day when the soil is soft helps minimise the shock effect transmitted throughout the human body … somewhat.

It was at this stage that I fell into contemplation on the miracle that is a seed. Each small disc, a tiny blueprint for the species I hope will emerge next spring, lifting helmeted heads of yellow above the soil while, down below, the roots are latching onto the underparts of the grasses, Timothy, Cock'sfoot or Couch, weakening them enough to allow spaces for other wildflowers to establish themselves.

A long winter passed. I found it hard not to spend hours combing through the sparse vegetation in early spring, looking for the first signs of the little plants. 'There's one, no, that's not it … But yes, that's it there … Small, sharply-pointed, darkish-green, with little jagged teeth along the margin … They're here!' They eventually arrived and the growth was most encouraging. By June the Yellow-rattle was established in several patches throughout the circle and I was well pleased.

That autumn, I gathered loads of seeds from my very own Yellow-rattle plants. Pete mowed the area, cutting it extremely short, making sure to remove the cuttings so that they didn't fertilise the soil. Then I sowed the

Meadow with Yellow-rattle and Cut-leaved Crane's-bill

Yellow-rattle seeds across the area in a similar manner to the previous year. I also collected the seeds of several other wildflowers which I thought might stand a chance of surviving – and some of them did. This was now 2014 and I was hoping that the following year there might be more wildflowers and fewer grasses, although some of the latter are truly handsome, my favourite being Yorkshire Fog with its feathery, pinkish plumes looking so elegant, especially as they sway in the light breeze.

The following year, 2015, turned out to be a very good year for the mini-meadow. The seeds had taken and shy visitors were spotted among the Yellow-rattle and the other plants that made this spot their home. One morning, I spied a young Greenfinch scuttle into it and imagined the warm buzzing, growing forest above his head hiding him from a marauding Magpie I had seen stealing a young Thrush the day before. Among the Yellow-rattle were many newcomers to the circle, shy-flowering pink **Cut-leaved Crane's-bill**, white **Common Mouse-ear**,

Tufted
Vetch

cylindrical purple heads of **Selfheal,** exquisite violet-coloured spikes of **Tufted Vetch**, feathery-leaved **Upright Hedge-parsley,** spreading heads of **Wild Carrot**, golden-yellow **Greater Bird's-foot Trefoil**, bright blue **Love-in-a-mist** – now what garden did that escape from? 'My' meadow was the best flowerbed I know. Later in the year, when the seedpods were rattling again, the area was absolutely full of Shield-bugs in various stages of their development. The bees were working up and down and around the circle's edge where Pete carefully mowed a clear path to delineate it. I took my little kneeler out, looking as if I was going to do a bit of work but I wasn't. I turned it upside down and instead I just sat on it and gazed. I was in heaven.

Perhaps I ought to mention a few dos and don'ts with regard to creating a wildflower patch. As stated, a sunny disposition is very important as is the soil – preferably unfertilised – if not, then best stripped back. Please don't be tempted to buy non-native seeds for this purpose. My best advice would be to collect your own seeds when they are ripe and quite dry – they usually go hard and dark in colour – and I find it a pleasant task, which helps me to learn more about different species and to recognise certain aspects of plant families. Yellow-rattle seeds must be sown in the autumn as they have to have time in the cold soil before they will germinate in spring. Collect seeds of other native wildflowers when they are dry also and sow them in small clumps where the earth is bare. I have been told that Yellow-rattle can take over, so I am watchful for

selfheal

this and if it happens I shall 'weed' it out as necessary. **Spear Thistles** and **Perennial Sow-thistles** have appeared in my patch, and I have lifted them and replanted them a little outside the area where the Goldfinch can happily visit them and feed on their gossamer-held seeds. I have also learned that leaving part of the patch uncut gives shelter to overwintering insects.

Creating a little wildflower patch for the first time is to start a love affair with a new part of the natural world. It's as if doors and windows open to give access to roomfuls of creatures and forms of life. Try it for yourself, please do.

Yellow-rattle | *Rhinanthus minor* | Gliográn

Cut-leaved Crane's-bill | *Geranium dissectum* | Crobh giobach

Selfheal | *Prunella vulgaris* | Duán ceannchosach

Tufted Vetch | *Vicia cracca* | Peasair na luch

Common Mouse-ear | *Cerastium fontanum* | Cluas luchóige mhara

Upright Hedge-parsley | *Torilis japonica* | Fionnas fáil

Wild Carrot | *Daucus carota* | Mealbhacán

Greater Bird's-foot-trefoil | *Lotus pedunculatus* | Crobh éin corraigh

Love-in-a-mist | *Nigella damascena* | Nigéal

Spear Thistle | *Cirsium vulgare* | Feochadán colgach

Perennial Sow-thistle | *Sonchus arvensis* | Bleachtán léana

SEPTEMBER IS ALSO a good month for harvesting berries such as those in our hedgerows. Any later and Blackberries will not be palatable, often being mildewed, full of maggots or, legend has it, they will have been spat on by Satan who was cast out of heaven by St Michael. Landing in Brambles, he is reputed to have put a curse on the fruit. St Michael's Day – or Michaelmas – is 29 September and after that day, one is counselled not to eat this fruit.

For whatever reason you prefer, it is perhaps best to avoid using them too late in the season but when they are fresh, plump and juicy there is really no other fruit that has such a rich, wonderful flavour. Some prefer to limit their intake of blackberries by only drinking it – Merlot is frequently enhanced with this fruit – but I have found other, more prudent ways of accessing its intense flavour. Can I share some with you, please?

In May, the many microspecies of **Bramble** – and there are close to 100 in Ireland – bear flowers that do their job of attracting pollinators by parading five crumpled pale pink or white petals around an abundant display of stamens. In autumn, the result of the pollination appears on most country hedgerows and succulent, juicy fruits are there for the picking. More correctly, a Blackberry is an aggregate fruit consisting of small drupelets or little circular berries, each containing a single seed. They are ready for use in so many ways, in tarts and pies, in jams and chutneys, and in ice creams and sorbets. I love to gather Blackberries and they give me a creative urge to do some cooking and, of course, eating. An excellent source of vitamin C, they also

Blackberries

bring many minerals to the table such as manganese, copper and potassium. As well as that, they have a marvellous, unmistakeable flavour and when they are being cooked, they give an incredible aroma that I find most evocative.

It reminds me of the time in my childhood when we used to take ourselves to the foothills of the Dublin Mountains and collect jam jars full of these wonderful fruits. Dad would tie string around the lip of the jars and create a loop that would hang on our small wrists so that we could use two hands to pluck the fruit off the spreading stems. As each of us filled our jam jars, the contents would be decanted into a larger container for transporting home. One of my own favourite recipes – and it is child's play – is for Blackberry and Apple jam.

jam on the way

Bramble | *Rubus fructicosus* | Dris

Blackberry and Apple Jam

Ingredients

500g/1lb 2oz
Blackberries

500g/1lb 2oz
cooking apples

Juice of one lemon

1 tablespoon water

1kg/2lb 3oz white
sugar

Method

Wash the blackberries carefully, putting the tiny bugs back into the garden and removing any rough or stony fruits.

Peel, core and thinly slice the apples.

Put the first four ingredients into a large pan over a low heat and bring slowly to the boil.

Simmer for about 15 minutes until the apples have 'exploded' and the berries are soft.

Add in the sugar, stirring as it melts, and then boil for about 10 minutes until it is getting thicker in consistency, stirring frequently so that it doesn't stick to the bottom of your pan. Try a little of the jam on a cooled saucer and when a little skin forms, it is ready.

Pour into jam jars that have been washed, dried and put into a moderate oven to sterilise. I let the jam jars get quite cold before putting on the lids.

The finished
product

COULD I EVER trust him again? After fifty years of marriage, to say nothing of the years of courting which went before, two beautiful children, more than 18,000 dinners, several tonnes of washing and ironing, and now this. It came as quite a shock. Well, decide for yourself.

It all began with a little dot on a map. The dot, more of a square really, told me that between the years 2000 and 2009, someone had seen an **Autumn Gentian** within a two-kilometre square – or tetrad as they are known in the business – just north of Ballyvaughan in County Clare. Words like needles and haystacks came to mind. Quite a small wildflower, quite a large square. It might not be that easy to find but I was there, the autumn sun was shining and I was going to give it a try. I had seen this little wildflower in Donegal in the late 1970s but not since and I had never photographed it. The books all agreed: dry grassland, sandy soil, calcareous dunes, these were its preferred habitats. Perhaps Bishop's Quarter, a long strip of beach with dunes leading up to some grassy turf where **Harebells** grew – that might be the right place to begin.

Harebell

I spent the morning mooching slowly along the grass bordering the dunes until I came to a field that was separated from me by an electric fence. There were cows in the field, each looking very morose. I don't like cows very much. They are large and forbidding and I usually try to avoid them, but there are times when I can be persuaded to drop the wimpy bit and be brave. I looked beyond the fence with my binoculars and – lo and behold – I spotted a clump of Autumn Gentians in the field. Very, very carefully I folded myself in two and wriggled below the wire, managing not to touch it. I was in. The cows never moved, just continued munching loudly. I walked slowly and quietly over to the Gentians and dropped to my knees. About a hand-span tall, they have pretty bell-shaped purple flowers, facing the sky, and they belong to the same family as the more widely known

Spring Gentians. They were such splendid little things and after many soundless 'Oohs' and 'Aahs', I took my photographs. These days it's so easy to check if your images are going to look all right and they seemed to be just what I wanted. I packed up my gear and wriggled out, unscathed. I was thoroughly delighted with my morning's work.

Over lunch, I told my dearly beloved all about it. He expressed a wish to see the Autumn Gentians, too, so I took him back and showed him the field behind the fence. He gently tipped the fence and assured me it was not 'live' at all. I hadn't needed to be so careful after all. I'm a trusting sort of person who until then believed every word he ever uttered. I stepped through the fence, quite casually this time, and with a sudden, horrible bang to my rear end, I was shot into the next parish. Nice assassination attempt, Pete!

Autumn Gentian | *Gentianella amarella* | Muilcheann

ANOTHER YUMMY use for Blackberries is to combine them with apples and make a tart. The quantities of pastry and fruit can vary depending on the size of your pie plate. These quantities are for a 25-centimetre/10-inch plate.

Blackberry and Apple Tart

Ingredients

225g/8 oz plain flour

Pinch of salt

100g/3½ oz butter

2–3 tablespoons cold water

400g/14 oz black-berries approximately

2 medium cooking apples

50g/2 oz white or caster sugar – or to taste

1 egg, beaten

To serve
cream, custard or ice cream

Method

Pre-heat oven to 375°F/Gas mark 5/190°C

Sieve the flour and salt into a large bowl.

Cut the butter into pieces and rub it into the flour until it looks like coarse breadcrumbs

Add in enough water to make a firm, not too wet, dough.

Wrap it in cling film and put it into the fridge while you prepare the fruit.

Wash the blackberries and drain them well. If they are too wet, the bottom of the tart will be soggy.

Peel and core the apples and slice them thinly.

Roll out the pastry on a lightly floured surface and lift it onto a greased tin, gently easing it into place, using your knuckles to press it into the bottom.

Cut away the excess dough, roll it thinly and cut it into strips long enough to cross the pie plate.

Prick the base lightly with a fork, then gently fit a circle of baking paper and one of foil into it.

Cover the rim of the tart lightly with baking paper.

Put into the oven on a hot baking sheet for 20 minutes.

Remove the pastry case from the oven and take out the foil and paper.

Return the pastry case to the oven for 7–10 minutes or until the crust is turning a little sand-coloured.

Spread half of the apple slices across the pastry case.

Sprinkle half the blackberries on top of the apple slices. Hold back a few blackberries to pop into the spaces between the pastry strips.

Spread the remaining apple slices and the rest of the blackberries into the case.

Sprinkle the sugar across the blackberries. Paint the rim of the tart with the beaten egg and 'weave' the pastry strips across the tart, sticking them to the rim of the pastry.

Paint all the pastry with beaten egg and sprinkle a little caster sugar across the pastry.

Place the remaining blackberries into the gaps in the woven pastry.

Place on a hot baking sheet in the oven and bake for about 40–50 minutes or until the pastry is cooked and the fruit is bubbling.

Serve with whipped cream, custard or ice cream – or all three.

Blackberry and
apple tart

Cottonweed – one of our Protected Species

Hanging on for dear life … that is probably the best way to describe the status of **Cottonweed** in the second decade of the twenty-first century. I wanted to see it but could never find it. About nine years ago my luck changed.

Pete and I were down in Tacumshin, that little piece of heaven on the south Wexford coast. We were watching some Marsh Harriers doing what they do best, drifting over the reed beds bordering this wetland, hunting for their food. We became aware that we were not the only observers of this phenomenon. We had been joined by another 'citizen scientist', equally excited at the spectacle. We got talking and exchanging information regarding special finds and sites in the area, both fauna and flora, and this kind person went on to tell us exactly where we might find

the Cottonweed. To me this was like winning the lottery and a few days later, we followed up, locating about twenty plants of this species.

Only just surviving, the plants are quite unusual in that the leaves and stems are covered in what resembles frosted, silvery down. At the top of the stems there are small flowerheads of tubular yellow florets. We have returned each year since and some years they would appear to be doing slightly better than others. This is a protected species under the Flora (Protection) Order, 2015, now found only in this one location, and every year, when we set out to look for it, we are afraid that it will have gone – finally disappearing from its one small home in Ireland. It is a horrible, chilling feeling to look at something you fear future generations may never see.

Cottonweed | *Achillea maritima* | Cluasach mhara

seen on the wing in september

Still to be found occasionally this month is the **Small Copper**, a small, brightly coloured species found in fields and hedgerows. Eggs laid singly on Common and Sheep's Sorrel. An adult is seen here feeding on Common Fleabane.

The **Grayling** wins all prizes for camouflage, closing its wings the instant it lands, blending into the rocky habitat by orienting towards the sun and casting its shadow. It flies in the Burren and in coastal areas where there is plenty of exposed rock. Its eggs are laid singly on grasses.

As a child, I knew all white butterflies as 'Cabbage Whites'. They were the bane of my mother's life as they laid their eggs on the plants of the Brassica (or cabbage) family she was doing her best to grow. I now know them a bit better, especially the more common varieties – the Large and the Small White. Briefly, the **Large White** differs from the Small White, not only in size but in the markings on its upper forewings. The dark markings extend further down the rear edge of the wing. The patches at the tip of the **Small White'**s forewings are a smudgy-grey with black at the extreme ends *only*. The Small White has a wingspan that is typically smaller than the Large White, but frustratingly they can overlap in size – you can have large Small Whites and small Large Whites! Unlike the Green-veined White (see page 214), the veins on their wings are not pigmented. They both fly in gardens, over arable crops and in wild places and are seen here feeding on a garden plant, *Inula hookeri*.

small Copper

Small White

Grayling

Large White

Hawthorn berries
or 'haws'

Deireadh Fómhair

October

October, originally the eighth month of the old Roman calendar, thus named from Latin 'octo' meaning eight • the second month of the Irish Meteorological service's autumn, it is thirty-one days long.

N HIS POEM 'AUTUMN', John Keats wrote of the season of mists and mellow fruitfulness and I have come to associate his 'Close bosom-friend of the maturing sun' with October.

Over the years I have learned, the hard way, never to leave the camera at home. So many times I've come across something worthy of a photographic record and called myself all kinds of stupid idiot for not having it with me. While the newfangled camera phones are not bad, I would always prefer to get the best image possible by using my 'real' camera, a trusted heavyweight DSLR. If I were to catalogue the species I have missed, it would be a long list. Instead, I will tell you about three little plant introductions to Ireland that I came across, happily, when I had the camera with me.

Species number one was found when I was on my way to visit a friend in Dublin's Mater Hospital. I walked up from O'Connell Street, past the Garden of Remembrance and up North Frederick Street. It was a lovely sunny morning and the dry streets were bright in the autumn sunshine, low, sharp shadows lying across the concrete pavements. On my left were some railings around ground that was home to an enormous tangled mess of empty crisp bags, drink cans, torn newspapers and other detritus of urban living. Through the muddle and chaos, a couple of stems were poking out, bearing clusters of pretty four-petalled yellow flowers. I didn't recognise them, except that I knew from their disposition that they had to belong to the Cabbage family. This is a massive group of plants known scientifically as Brassicaceae, one of the families that help to feed the world. When we eat vegetables such as sprouts, cauliflower, cabbage or broccoli or if we cook with rapeseed oil, we are consuming some products from this large family. I looked more closely and saw that there were quite unusually long seedpods and lance-shaped leaves with a single pair of narrow side lobes.

I considered the scene before me, trying to work out how I could possibly get a few respectable photographs of the plants, growing where they were, but there was no way. The tangle and clutter would make nothing but a jumbled, useless image. What could I do? I walked slowly up the street and then I noticed that one plant was stretching itself out through the railings, a foot or so above the pavement. It was out on its own, demanding my attention. As the plants grew in such abundance, I didn't feel too bad about quickly snapping off one long stem, just above the ground, and, holding it close to my side, I swiftly moved on. I crossed the road at the top and made my way to a bus shelter where I sat, unobtrusively, taking photographs of the various parts of the plant while holding it at arm's length, a trick I had learned over the years. It worked. The images were enough to enable me to make my identification and the specimens were pressed later for confirmation purposes.

My new find was **Eastern Rocket**, an annual plant that found its way to Ireland from Asia and North Africa. It has been here for over a century, but does not seem to have spread too widely. The term 'introduction' is used where a plant species has arrived in Ireland accidentally, whether by man or by bird, or, as is often the case, by being imported as a garden plant. It is only when the plants become a nuisance and threaten our native species that they are termed 'invasive aliens' and this is clearly not the case with Eastern Rocket. This was a good find.

A few weeks later, Pete and I decided we needed a new bed. That's a bit of a non sequitur, I know, but it leads me on to how I came across my next introduced species, this time in a Dublin suburb, Sallynoggin, close to the port of Dún Laoghaire. Not a very good location for spotting nature, you might think, this built-up area of large retail buildings, builders' providers, kitchen-fittings outlets

Eastern Rocket

and other shops. However, as we passed across the front of the furniture shop, my subconscious radar registered something different and, a few paces later, I stopped in my tracks, and went into reverse. There it was, growing out of a crack between the wall and the pavement, a straggly plant with tiny greenish-yellow flowers on a long spike, narrow, shiny leaves completing the picture. I had never seen this species before and my priorities are set in stone. The bed could wait. The camera was in the backpack and out it came.

This proved to be an interesting plant, **Annual Mercury**, which was recorded in Ireland as far back as 1794 when it was growing 'plentifully in waste and cultivated ground' according to botanist Nathaniel Colgan in his 1904 *Flora of the County Dublin*. He wrote that, 'Its present limits are Balbriggan on the north, Killiney on the south, and Blanchardstown on the west. Within these limits, however, its distribution is by no means continuous.' Since those words were written over 100 years ago, Annual

Annual
Mercury

Mercury has spread beyond the Pale and is now found in Counties Cork, Waterford, Wexford and Kilkenny, with a couple of stragglers elsewhere in the country.

The third urban species I found was growing under the railway bridge on Dublin's Westland Row, across the road from Pearse Station. I was on my way to the National Botanic Gardens in Glasnevin and had come into the city by DART. I always take the No. 4 bus to the Gardens, from Westland Row, so I'd crossed the road and as I waited for the bus, I scanned the tops of the walls and the cracks in the pavements for signs of vegetation. My curiosity was rewarded. Among the dust and cigarette butts were several hairy, sticky-leaved plants with white flowers, each with five, toothed petals in a circle around a yellow disc – not unlike a small daisy. These intriguing little plants had found their foothold in the cracks at street level and although they were covered in dust, I thought it worth getting a photo or two as I had no notion what they might be. Kicking away the cigarette

shaggy-soldier

butts and ignoring the odd glances of passers-by, I got to work. I found out later that this was a species from Mexico, which has only been in Ireland since the late 1990s and probably is what is known as a garden escape. It grows on arable land in other countries and can cause havoc with crops but, so far, not here. It is commonly known as **Shaggy-soldier**. The area in which I found it is regularly used by homeless people at night, the space between the supporting bridge columns giving them some small shelter. I have also seen them sleeping in the daytime, while the 'suits' pass by, their ears muted to the sounds around, tuned into the background music of their own lives. Each poor sleeper seemed to me to be another sort of poor 'shaggy soldier', fighting a hard battle, close to losing his own war.

Eastern Rocket | *Sisymbrium orientale* | Maol Íosa
Annual Mercury | *Mercurialis annua* | Lus glinne beag
Shaggy-soldier | *Galinsoga quadriradiata*

NAVELWORT, NIPPLEWORT, Toothwort – funny names, I used to think. What have they in common, I wondered. Well, their names all end in the word 'wort' – which comes from the Old English '*wyrt*' for herb or root – but that's not the only answer. Each of these is one of the many species that once lent weight to the theory behind the 'Doctrine of Signatures'.

Briefly, the Doctrine of Signatures was a concept introduced into medicine in the 1500s. In the words of sixteenth-century botanist and philosopher Paracelsus, the belief was that 'Nature marks each growth … according to its curative benefit'. He held that God marked everything he created with some sign that would help to direct healers towards finding cures for ailments. For example, when he looked at

Navelwort

Nipplewort

the leaf of one plant species – *Umbilicus rupestris* – he saw a resemblance to a human navel and applied the doctrine. Perhaps unsurprisingly, this species became commonly known as **Navelwort**. The renowned seventeenth-century herbalist Nicholas Culpeper wrote that 'the juice … being drank is very effectual … to cool a fainting hot stomach … or the bowels'.

Among the species included in this doctrine was **Nipplewort**, a yellow-flowered, straggly plant of waste places, which has very small, nipple-like buds. This plant was traditionally used in the treatment of breast ulcers, on sore nipples in nursing mothers and, when necessary, to curtail the flow of breast milk.

The juice extracted from **Eyebright** was used to create eyedrops in order to cure all sorts of eye problems. This wildflower has exquisite white, lilac-tinted flowers which some believed looked like little eyes. Culpeper wrote: 'If the herb was but as much used as it is neglected, it would half spoil the spectacle maker's trade.'

There were many other species that were used in herbal medicine following the Doctrine of Signatures and some of these medications would

Little Celandine

appear to be valued still. The yellow-flowered harbinger of spring, **Lesser Celandine**, was traditionally known to herbalists as **Pilewort** as its roots contain small knobbly nodules. Culpeper wrote: 'If you dig up the root of it, you shall perceive the perfect image of the disease which they commonly call the piles'. The roots were made into an ointment to help reduce the pain of haemorrhoids and I know that this remedy was still being made in County Roscommon a decade ago.

Another species whose common name ends in 'wort' is **Heath Milkwort**. It acquired its name through its reputation for enhancing the milk of cows that grazed on it. Whenever I see that flower, I remember an early October day, some years ago, when I was in Wicklow, the Garden County, on a path that winds its way up Brockagh. At any time of the year it's a lovely walk, one that gives a feeling of being on top of the world for a relatively small effort, something that suits my lethargic nature very well. Brockagh – *Sliabh na Brocaí* ('mountain of the badgers') – lies just a short distance from the village of Laragh and has long been a favourite place, especially outside the summer months, in a time when the hills are quieter and 'peace comes dropping slow'.

I wanted to get a photograph of Heath Milkwort, which was growing close to the forestry path at the lower part of the hill. This is by no means a rare species but it is extremely pretty and to show its intricacies, a really close-up image is necessary. At that stage, I didn't have one. The flowers of Heath Milkwort are small, generally deep blue, although occasionally pink. They appear to have two wing-like petals, which are in fact sepals, those parts of the plant that protect the flower when in bud. The flower itself is a small tube of three fused petals, which have pretty, fringed margins.

Heath
Milkwort

On the path in a Beech wood at Laragh

It was a little late in the season for this species but it was in very good shape and so it was worth a photograph. Heath Milkwort being a plant of short stature, the only thing for me to do was to lie down flat on the path and hold the camera steady, resting my elbows on the ground in front of me. The light was just right, there was a tiny lull in the breeze as I settled down and, bracing my arms, I carefully framed the image. Just as I was about to press the shutter release, I heard a loud roar coming from further up the path. I looked up and saw two young men running towards me. As they got closer, they slowed down. 'Oh my God! We thought you were dead,' one of them said, 'we got such a fright.' They were both quite shaken and it took me some time to reassure them that all was well.

I told them what I was doing and thanked them for their concern and solicitude. When their heart rates seemed to have returned to normal, we shook hands and they made their way down the track. By the time they had gone, so had the perfect lighting conditions and the breeze was stirring again. It was a small loss when set against the kindness of these strangers. The photograph could wait for another day.

Navelwort | *Umbilicus rupestris* | **Cornán caisil**

Nipplewort | *Lapsana communis* | Duilleog Bhríde

Eyebright | *Euphrasia officinalis* | Glanrosc

Lesser Celandine | *Ficaria verna* | Grán arcáin

Heath Milkwort | *Polygala serpyllifolia* | Na deirfiúríní

I SUPPOSE SOME could call it an obsession. If something is growing anywhere, be it a crack in a wall or through a grating in a pavement, I always want to examine it, just to see what it is. I can never ignore vegetation. This particular walk was no different.

Tintern Abbey was built in the thirteenth century, on the western shore of Bannow Bay, County Wexford, by William Marshal, Earl of Pembroke and Lord of Leinster. During a voyage to Ireland, which almost became a catastrophic shipwreck, he had vowed that, if saved from a watery grave, he would found an abbey in gratitude. The man was true to his word and the abbey was built on a south-facing slope a short distance upstream from the spot where he had been safely delivered. A Cistercian abbey, it was named after Tintern Abbey in Wales, of which Marshal was patron. Some time after the Dissolution of the Monasteries in Ireland in 1537, the abbey became home to the Colclough family, from whom it passed in the 1960s and it is now in the care of the Office of Public Works.

Tintern is a place Pete and I visit regularly, walking along the pathways through the grounds, admiring the **Bluebells,** which, along with **Early-purple Orchids** and **Lords-and-ladies**, crowd the woodland floor in springtime. However, on this particular day, there was a surprise in store for me as we strolled towards the sixteenth-century bridge spanning the river that flows to the sea at Saltmills.

The ground falls away gently from the abbey towards the paved pathway we were taking. In this slope are three large rectangular ponds where I had previously encountered quite a few interesting and not-too-common species of

Lords-and-ladies

wildflowers. Earlier in the year **Monkeyflower** had shone out gaudily from the tangle of vegetation at the border of one of the ponds, providing bright splashes of yellow flowers, each sprinkled with a few tiny red dots. Not a native species, its origins are in North America where it also likes to grow in marshy, damp places.

Monkey-flower

As I passed the lowest pond, something caught my eye, something small and yellow. I walked across the grass to get a better look, but the small yellow something – and several more besides – was too far away to see clearly. I borrowed Pete's binoculars and when I focused on these small yellow dots, I was absolutely certain that I had never seen them or anything like them before. The familiar excitement took over – something like Christmas Eve as a child, the stocking at the end of the bed, hopes high as a house.

There was only one thing to do. Removing my shoes and socks, I rolled up the bottoms of my trousers and, seating myself on the grass, I shuffled myself closer to the pond, dropping my feet into the warm water. The ground below my feet was soft and sandy, the camera was safe, held aloft as I moved slowly through the vegetation, towards the yellow dots.

Imagine you are holding an **Oxeye** or **Dog Daisy** and playing the game we loved to play as youngsters – 'He loves me, he loves me not'. You have plucked all the white 'petals' off the flower head and you are left with, not only your answer, be it good or bad, but also a little yellow button. This yellow dome contains what are known in botanical circles as 'disc florets' or tiny little individual flowers, all clustered into a tight bunch. That was exactly what this flower looked like. The little buttons were held upright, on straight, stout stems, like little yellow-topped knitting needles, poking up and sharing their space in the pond with other water-loving species. The stems were reddish and were clasped at regular intervals by sheathing leaves. As I took my photographs, I tried to recall if I had ever seen illustrations or photographs of this species in my flower guides but nothing came to mind.

The warm water was gentle, even silky, and the bottom of the pond was pleasant to walk on as I moved back towards the bank. I climbed out, experiencing that sensuous feel of the soft, slightly damp sward under my feet, insoles being gently tickled by the blunted grass, toes spread wide released from the confines of shoes, a slightly wicked pleasure rising from them. I rubbed my feet on the grass to dry them off a bit, and put my socks and shoes back on. I could feel the thrill of finding something new and unexpected, the anticipation of making an identification. After some turning of pages and going through several flower guides, my find turned out to be **Buttonweed**. Far from its homeland in South Africa, it was introduced into some parts of Europe but nobody knows how it came to be where I found it on that warm and sunny October morning in 2008. I could never discover how it had made its way into the pond in Tintern. Although I contacted the Office of Public Works to see whether it had been consciously planted, the answer was no, it must have made its way all by itself.

Button-weed

And now for a footnote to that story: when I got home, Pete suggested to me that I should give my feet a good wash. I wondered why he felt it necessary to say this to me and queried his suggestion. He reckoned that the pond I had been paddling in was nothing other than a filter bed for treating the outflow from the abbey's visitor's centre, café and restrooms. Whoops.

Bluebell | *Hyacinthoides non-scripta* | Coinnle corra
Early-purple Orchid | *Orchis mascula* | Magairlín meidhreach
Lords-and-ladies | *Arum maculatum* | Cluas chaoin
Monkeyflower | *Mimulus guttatus* | Buí an bhogaigh
Oxeye Daisy | *Leucanthemum vulgare* | Nóinín mór
Buttonweed | *Cotula coronopifoli* | Cnaipin

Great
Willowherb

samhain

November

eleventh month of the year in the
Julian and Gregorian Calendars •
last month of meteorological
autumn in Ireland

NOVEMBER IS THE TIME OF YEAR when I usually sort out the photographs taken over the previous few months. Tending to keep any image that might be useful in the future, the theory is that I record where they are in my sprawling filing system and delete all the duds. It is a nice task and in my mind I revisit the places where the images were taken and the people I was with. Funny stories are sometimes attached, and I love looking at these pictures of the wildflowers, reminding myself of how much pleasure they have given to me.

I set out, several decades ago, to try to photograph whatever wildflower species I came across and keep a log of when and where I had located it first. The result of a combination of overlapping pleasures gradually built up to a large quantity of photographic prints, then 35mm slides and finally, when the digital age arrived, it became a sizeable collection on a plethora of hard drives and, now, cloud storage. In tandem with the photographic process, I tried to learn as much as I could about the species themselves. I spent winter months swotting up on botanical knowledge through as many books as I could get my hands on. I also attended lectures and courses wherever they were available, trying to bring that newly acquired information into the field the following year.

But, before all of this began to grow, twin seeds were sown: one was to germinate as a passion for wildflowers and the other grew into a lifelong interest in and love of photography and it is the development of this latter pursuit I would like to enlarge upon here. When I was a child, our home had a semi-basement room running the width of the house, separated into two large windowless rooms. Like a cellar, not intended for habitation, the entire space was imaginatively named 'The Underneath' and half of it was probably what might now be called a utility room. In one corner our bikes were stacked, the coal was heaped in another corner behind a low wooden wall, and there was a sink and a loo behind the door. But it was in the other half that my imagination took flight.

My father was a very gifted photographer and he had converted this half of 'The Underneath' into his hobby space and darkroom. As there

white
bluebell

Top left: Kodak six-20 Junior; top right: Kodak Brownie 127;
bottom: Nikon D7100 with Nikon 18-300mm lens

were no windows in this part of the house, it was easy to keep light out and I spent so many happy hours with him, watching images gradually come to life in his developing and printing dishes. The smell of the chemicals was addictive as was the strange red glow of the overhead light, which sent a magic cast across the room. Dad had a large black enlarger and into this he would insert a negative and, somehow, he would always know how long to allow the light from the enlarger to play through the negative and on to the sensitive photographic paper. If there was an area he wanted to hold back, he would wave his closed fingers across the beam, 'dodging' the light. In contrast, he would give an increased amount of light to a paler area by 'burning' it in and not allowing the same intensity to reach other parts of the image. These terms – dodging and burning – have now come into digital image parlance. I wonder how many know their origins – probably a bit like 'cut' and 'paste' were words previously used in the printing houses' lexicon.

My father's photographic journey took him through several technologies. It began with a plate camera, which used a thin glass plate, coated with an emulsion of silver salts on which the image was taken. This medium gave an excellent image but photographic film gradually became a more popular choice, first black and white, then colour. Like most photographers, he amassed several cameras but his favourite in latter days was an Olympus. I wonder what he would have made of the digital camera, let alone camera phones.

My own journey started around the age of ten when my Uncle Bernie gave me a Kodak Brownie 127. It produced small black-and-white images. I loved it. Later I progressed from a Praktica through the Nikon range of cameras, first on 35mm film, then digital, trying to learn and focus on the new adaptations of the old technology. I think my favourite end product is still the 35mm slide.

I love the moment I press the shutter release. The optimism is perpetual. It never goes away. I'm always hoping the next image will be the best yet. I'm amused by the name given to one current imaging programme – Lightroom – mirroring the early days when the darkroom was the place where the exciting part of the process developed. Downloading a clatter of images onto a computer can never replace the magic of the darkroom. The smell of the chemicals is missing, the eerie red light, the slow pace and the painstaking route to creating a perfect, unique image – they're all gone. I know that I could never afford to take all the images I take these days if I was still paying for film stock. It is also so much easier now for anyone to take photographs. Perhaps I'm being a dinosaur, but I think a large bank of skills has been lost and so many will never appreciate the true art and craft of photography.

WHILE I'M FILING away my memories
and images, I sometimes see patterns
emerging. Some years, all of the flowers
have bloomed a week or so earlier than
usual; sometimes I notice that many of
the images also depict butterflies
or other insects feeding on the
flowers' nectar – was that perhaps
a good butterfly year? Twice I

Cross-leaved
Heath

Meadow
saffron

have noticed a strange phenomenon – many of the wildflowers have produced unexpected white blossoms.

Perhaps I should explain – what I mean is that I have found several white versions of a wildflower that is normally another colour. One year I photographed a white-flowering **Great Willowherb** (normally pink), **Ivy-leaved Toadflax** (lilac – see page 25), **Bush Vetch** (purple) and **Selfheal** (violet-purple). Another year it was a white **Foxglove** (pink), **Bluebell** (blue) (see page 259), **Cross-leaved Heath** (magenta) and the incredibly beautiful white version of **Meadow Saffron** (pink); and you may have read earlier about the white **Bee Orchid** we found in the Burren one June (see page 83). Some anomalies have given rise to superstition such as white Heather being lucky, a fourth leaf on a clover also considered to be a sign of imminent fortune but so far I sadly can't confirm those beliefs.

Great Willowherb | *Epilobium hirsutum* | Lus na Tríonóide

Ivy-leaved Toadflax | *Cymbalaria muralis* | Buaflíon balla

Bush Vetch | *Vicia sepium* | Peasair fhiáin

Selfheal | *Prunella vulgaris* | Duán ceannchosach

Foxglove | *Digitalis purpurea* | Lus mór

Bluebell | *Hyacinthoides non-scripta* | Coinnle corra

Cross-leaved Heath | *Erica tetralix* | Fraoch naoscaí

Meadow Saffron | *Colchicum autumnale* | Cróch an fhómhair

Blackthorn

One of nature's delights that has come to be a regular winter feature in our house is Sloe Gin – often referred to as Looney Soup, due to its ability to render an over-embiber totally silly. It's one of those sneaky drinks – all sweet and syrupy going down, but with a kick to it when you try to stand up. Like most good things in life, the direction is 'to be taken in moderation only', if you know what I mean.

In early spring, the **Blackthorn** hedges produce dense spikes of snowy-white flowers on dark, spiny branches, each flower's five petals encircling an outstanding crop of long, white, orange-tipped stamens. Then, several months later, those flowers have become small, damson-like fruits. Best picked after the first frost, they can then be made into an absolutely gorgeous red liqueur. This is the recipe we always use:

Blackthorn | *Prunus spinosa* | Draighean

Sloe Gin

Collect 200g/7oz sloes, ensuring they are ripe by pressing them between your finger and thumb. If they are soft and give a bit, they are ready. Put them into the freezer overnight.

sloes

Next day take a large preserving jar such as a Kilner. Pour into it 500ml/18fl oz/ 1 pint of gin. Add 100g/3½oz white sugar and the frozen sloes. Secure the lid of the jar and lay it on its side in a cold, dark place.

Every other day for a couple of months, give the jar a good shake to help the sugar to dissolve. Then let it settle for as long as you can contain your patience – a few more months would be good.

Wash and sterilise two or three small, sealable bottles, a small funnel and some fine muslin by boiling them for 5 minutes (remove the bottles' rubber seals before doing this and wash them well in hot soapy water). When the bottles are completely cold, pour the liquor through the muslin and funnel into the bottles. Keep them in a cool, dark place until you are ready to taste them. And beware, the flavour makes this liquid quite addictive!

The resulting tipple

THE DARK MONTHS of the year are good times for reading up on our botanical treasures, and trying to understand more about the history of the plants we have. Among those are the Lusitanian species, also known as the Hiberno–Cantabrian flora.

This is a unique collection of fifteen wild-flower species that are thought to have come to Ireland from the Mediterranean and the Iberian Peninsula at a time when the island of Ireland was still physically joined to Britain and continental Europe. The group is generally absent from our neighbouring island and includes species as varied as **Kerry Lily** (see page 137), **Dense-flowered Orchid**, **St Dabeoc's Heath** (see page 204) and **Strawberry-tree**. These are found mostly in the west and south-west regions of Ireland. There are also species belonging to the arctic/alpine group, which includes **Mountain Avens** (see page 114), and there are other rarities such as the minuscule **Bog Orchid**, a tiny Orchid that can reproduce itself not only by pollen but by means of tiny bulbils growing along the margins of its leaves which detach themselves when fully developed and drop into the bog.

If this latter little plant were a soldier, he − or she − would

strawberry-tree

Dense-flowered orchid

Bog
Orchid

Bird's-nest
Orchid

be in most effective camouflage gear, blending in with the mosses and rushes in the marshy ground that is its habitat. To find this species means you must sink slowly into swampy ground whilst trying to see where you are putting your wellied feet, all the while endeavouring to stay upright. I wonder if this species is as rare as its distribution map would make it appear. It grows to about 12 centimetres high and its colour, honey-greeny-yellow, blends in extremely well with the terrain. This is not where one might choose to walk unless there was a good reason, such as a botanical hunt. I was first shown it by a friend of a similar age to myself and it was only because we had a younger person with us that we didn't get stuck in that bog permanently. Having crouched down to look at it closely, we both sank more than a little and neither of us found it easy to get back out.

Also classed as 'rare' is **Bird's-nest Orchid**, a honey-coloured saprophyte, which means that it has no green chlorophyll but takes its

Round-leaved Wintergreen

nutrition from decomposing vegetation, using thread-like filaments attached to its roots. I first saw this species in the Dolomites in Italy and it was to be three decades before I saw it in Ireland, its strange ghostly appearance hidden in the darkness of a beech wood where it stood, leafless and erect through the leaf litter.

The Flora (Protection) Order, 2015 makes it 'illegal to cut, uproot or damage the listed species in any way', or to offer them for sale. This prohibition extends to the taking or sale of seed. The list includes many flowering plants, lichens, ferns,

Oysterplant

mosses, liverworts and stoneworts. Among those named is a **Wintergreen** subspecies that grows in County Wexford, **Betony** in Kerry and Wexford, and **Oysterplant**, which is found in a few northern coastal locations. I would never have seen some of these species nor the beautiful **Green-winged Orchid** (see page ii), now classed as 'Vulnerable', had it not been for the kindness of my botanical friends Christine Cassidy, Howard Frost, Paul Green, Jackie O'Connell, Ulli Peiler, Paddy Tobin and Christopher Wilson (now sadly deceased).

Betony

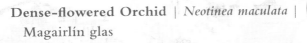

Dense-flowered Orchid | *Neotinea maculata* | Magairlín glas

Strawberry-tree | *Arbutus unedo* | Caithne

Bog Orchid | *Ophrys apifera* | Magairlín na mbeach

Bird's-nest Orchid | *Neottia nidus-avis* | Magairlín neide éin

Round-leaved Wintergreen | *Pyrola rotundifolia* subsp. *maritima* | Glasluibh chruinn

Betony | *Betonica officinalis* | Lus beatha

Oysterplant | *Mertensia maritima* | Lus na sceallaí

Green-winged (or Green-veined) Orchid | *Anacamptis morio* | Magairlín féitheach

Ivy-covered trees in the Raven, County Wexford

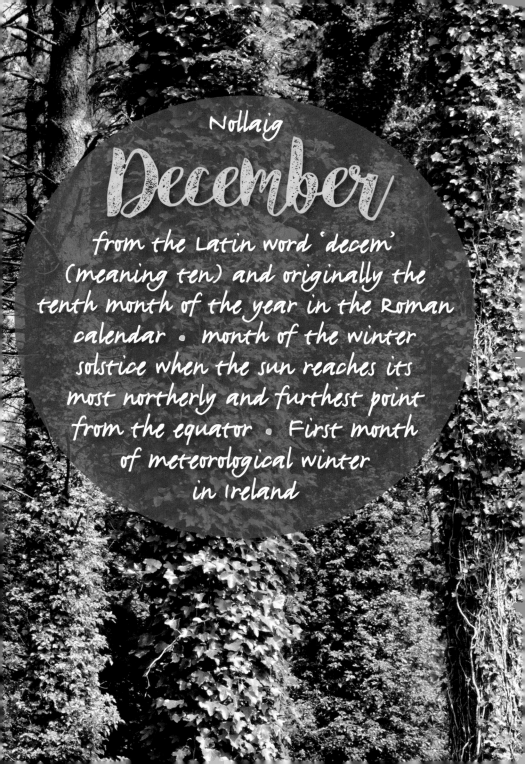

Nollaig

December

from the Latin word 'decem' (meaning ten) and originally the tenth month of the year in the Roman calendar • month of the winter solstice when the sun reaches its most northerly and furthest point from the equator • First month of meteorological winter in Ireland

Holly
berries

The holly and the ivy,
When they are both full grown,
Of all trees that are in the wood,
The holly bears the crown.

Holly
flowers

THOUGHTS OF DECEMBER bring back images of our '**Holly** walks' when we used to take an annual trip to a spot where we knew this native tree grew and we'd cut a few sprigs for decorating the house at Christmas. We no longer follow this ritual because, with a growing appreciation of the fragility of our environment, we realise that Holly needs to be allowed to grow, undamaged, to provide for creatures other than humans. During winter, birds take refuge in Holly trees, whose spiny leaves, shining in winter's low light, afford the birds a degree of protection from predators. The lower leaves – and those of the younger trees – are sharply prickled, the upper leaves smooth with wavy margins; this means that the lower parts are protected from being overbrowsed by animals. After the first frost, the red berries become soft and provide food for birds and small animals such as wood mice. These berries have grown from the tiny white flowers that bloomed in May and June, the female and male flowers occurring on separate trees. Hedgehogs use the thick leaf litter below Holly trees as places to pass their winter in hibernation, and the Holly Blue butterfly lays her eggs below the flower buds in spring.

Considered by the druids to be a sacred tree, traditionally Holly was also thought to offer protection from lightning strikes, with trees being planted close to dwellings to safeguard them.

Holly | *Ilex aquifolium* | Cuileann

Ivy growing on an old wall in Dalkey, County Dublin

A FEW DECEMBERS AGO, I was out for a different sort of 'Holly walk': it had changed its name to an '**Ivy** walk'. I was armed with a pair of secateurs and a large plastic bag. Once again, wanting to decorate the house for Christmas, I just needed to gather a few stems of Ivy. It was cold, the vapour off my breath drifting in front of me. I stooped to cut the Ivy close to the ground, thinking that I might be doing my good deed for the day by releasing a tree from some of the tight bonds encircling it. With the abundance of Ivy in this country, I didn't think I was causing any harm, but I suddenly got the feeling I was being watched. A young man stood a few feet away, an odd look on his face.

'It seems very strange to see you cutting that plant,' he said in an accent that told me he wasn't Irish and with a manner I found quite challenging.

'Why ever not?' I replied, feeling slightly uncomfortable and without any idea of what was going to come next. Was I going to be the subject of tomorrow's tabloid headlines?

'Well, it's just that where I come from, we don't do that. This plant is treasured because she is rare and I find it very hard to watch her being cut, as you are doing.'

I relaxed, a bit, and explained to him that it was far from rare in Ireland, in fact there are many who would like to see much less of it as it has a bad, somewhat undeserved, name for destroying masonry and trees. He was surprised but seemed to accept what I said. With near perfect English, he told me came from Poland. He had only been in Ireland for a couple of days, sorting out a job transfer with an Internet company and as it was the weekend, he had decided to take a bus, any bus, and see where it took him.

Drone fly on ivy

He'd been lucky in his choice of transport – the St Kevin's bus, a long-established service operating between Dublin city and Glendalough. As a child, I travelled this route with my father, several times, on our visits to see my Auntie Gladys in her house overlooking the monastic city's Lower Lake. At that time, the old softly sprung coach we took bounced and bobbed across the Calary bog. It was like riding along on a marshmallow. I always loved gazing out of the window, my father telling me the names of some of the Wicklow Mountains – the Sugar Loaf, Djouce and Scarr among them.

The young man told me that his plan was to go for a good long walk as he needed to clear his head after a few intense days. 'Nature always does it for me,' he said and seemed to take comfort from his own words. And that was how he found himself close to Laragh, a couple of miles from Glendalough in County Wicklow, where I was cutting Ivy.

I suppose if I was abroad and saw someone picking, for instance, **Spring Gentians** or **Bird's-nest Orchids** – both rare in Ireland – I would feel the same concern, even if they were growing in abundance.

Our meeting turned into one of those pleasant, unexpected episodes, and I enjoyed hearing about Poland's biodiversity. He told me that since 1989, when the communist era ended, there has been increased awareness of the environment but there are still many major problems. As long as coal-fired power plants continue to emit sulphur dioxide, habitats such as forests – which cover one third of the country – are being seriously degraded. These power plants contribute to around 90 per cent of Poland's energy but they are responsible for causing acid rain and subsequent harm to plants and animals. We strolled for a while, exchanging information about our two countries, and then I left him to enjoy his head-clearing walk.

I must admit I have a lot of time for Ivy. It is very giving when it comes to other forms of wildlife. Holly Blue butterflies lay their late summer eggs on Ivy as well as Holly, birds feed on its berries and the Brimstone butterfly is known to overwinter in its shelter. Its flowers – small yellow-green with five pointed petals and five projecting stamens – also provide a source of nectar for late-flying insects such as the drone fly in the picture (see page 275). Like the Holly, it has two forms of leaves. The early leaves are quite clearly three or five-lobed, dark green with pale veins, whereas the more mature leaves are often heart-shaped and very shiny.

Atlantic Ivy | *Hedera hibernica* | Eidhneán

To TAKE A WALK along one of the most northerly parts of the Burren, known as the Flaggy Shore, is an exhilarating experience at any time of the year. In the summer, tussocks of **Thrift** and clusters of **Common Bird's-foot-trefoil** paint the spaces between the rocks with splashes of pink and yellow. But in the harsher days of winter, when the vegetation has gone to ground, waiting for lighter days, there are still stories to be read from the rocks beneath our feet. These stories are held within the myriad of fossils.

Common Bird's-foot-trefoil and Thrift

Crinoid fossils

Fossil of coral branches in cross section

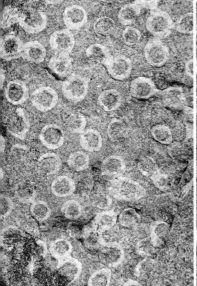

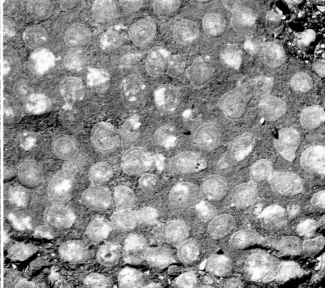

Fossils – memories in stone, older than our imagination can dream of, mute witnesses to the centuries, sealed in layers of strata that slowly raised themselves, sculpting the contours of continents, little by little. Crushed beneath a mass of sand, each grain itself is a distant remembrance of the land to which it once belonged. Traces of organisms, their remains slowly fading, dissolving, are replaced by minute particles. Over millennia their long-forgotten shapes are slowly reproduced, becoming petrified replicas of those vanished forms. Reed beds by the shores of the southern hemisphere's mighty oceans, thousands of generations later are locked in the grey limestone of the Flaggy Shore. At one time fan-shaped, coral is now a lace-like network in stone, uncovered by the Atlantic's persistent power. Here also are crinoids, small animals whose skeletons break into rings, leaving fragments, forever set in stone.

We behold our own passage through time as a life of transformation, of expansion of mind and body, more often everyday than epic. Our short years are regulated by the departure of each season, the baton passing from father to son, mother to daughter; wisdom, understanding, knowledge, each dispensed, filtered, questioned, altered or clasped to our hearts. But we will never know all the secrets stored within those stones. They are the voiceless observers of our sea-dwelling ancestors' odyssey as they crawled from their life in the deep, onto the shores, and evolved, giving us our breath.

County Clare's
Flaggy Shore

Thrift | *Armeria maritima* | Rabhán
Common Bird's-foot-trefoil | *Lotus corniculata* | Crobh éin

CHRISTMAS IN OUR house would not be the same without **Mistletoe**. The warm, friendly ritual of kissing under it is honoured, over and over, and nobody ever seems to decline. Perhaps they are all being incredibly polite or maybe they know that this eighteenth-century tradition ordains that anybody refusing a kiss would have bad luck visited upon them. I have also heard that, with every kiss, a berry should be removed from the sprig hanging overhead, and that when all the berries are gone, that's it — no more kissing. That's one part of the tradition we never intend to honour, but then, we are incurable romantics.

A ball of Mistletoe

Mistletoe is a strange species. Its scientific name is *Viscum album*; usually bird-distributed, the seeds are covered in a sticky, viscous gel that attaches itself to the bark of a tree. A 'hemiparasite' or partial parasite, it usually grows on branches of species such as apple, lime, poplar, willow and hawthorn. It is an evergreen, forming large, spherical masses of vegetation attached to the host tree by a structure called a *haustorium*. This is a root that penetrates the outer tissue of the host tree and draws out nutrients and water, causing damage to the host tree by reducing its growth. Birds are responsible for spreading the seeds, either by passing them through their guts or by wiping their sticky beaks onto trees. The Mistle Thrush acquired its common name by being one of those birds that favours a diet containing these seeds.

I had always read that in early spring, very small inconspicuous flowers form tight clusters, male and female, on separate plants, but I had never seen them. They are obviously very high up in trees so getting a photograph of one was not going to be an easy task. My friends at the National Botanic Gardens in Glasnevin had directed me to the relevant Poplar trees where I took photographs of the balls of vegetation but the flowers were way out of

Mistletoe
flowers

Mistletoe leaves and berries at the National Botanic Gardens, Glasnevin

reach. Luckily, there was one particular Hawthorn tree that was playing host to Mistletoe and it didn't have the height of the Poplars. On a cold March day in 2016, I eventually got to see and photograph my first Mistletoe flowers. I had reached up as high as I possibly could and gently pulled a twig towards the camera – and yes, they are absolutely minuscule – only two millimetres across with four triangular, greeny-yellow petals. They sit in small clusters between oblong leathery leaves, arranged like wings, opposite one another. By Christmas, the flowers will have been pollinated – by something very tiny, I suspect – and the plants will have loads of shiny, waxy, white berries, ready for our amorous custom to take place beneath them.

Mistletoe | *Viscum album* | Drualus

As EACH YEAR DRAWS to a close, there's a sense of impending dormancy, of nature going to ground, hibernating. Fortunately, this mood is transient, being gradually replaced by a feeling of anticipation, expectation and optimism. For so long I have been visited, far too early, by an annual desire to get out, to see for myself what nature is doing to the world outside. Sometimes it has dealt harshly with our environment and now it is difficult to know what we may expect from one year to the next. But we who love nature are blessed with this pursuit. The question is, how can we so-called 'citizen scientists' inspire younger generations to follow the paths we chose – to learn about, to love and to cherish our biodiversity?

I was lucky. Inspiration came to me from various sources. As a child, I have no idea why but I was drawn towards the 'weeds' in our garden, finding in them so many questions I needed to have answered. The 'hows' and 'whys' formed a long, colourful string of beads that would encircle and decorate my life.

Those little 'weeds' were not put there by man or woman, as were the Delphiniums and Dahlias in our flowerbeds. They just arrived and found their own niche and got on with their business. Dr Kathleen Lynn showed me that first Heath Spotted-Orchid which, while adding to the curiosity already present, gave birth to a mighty sense of awe and triggered a lifetime's passion. Other relatives, Winifred Wynne and Gladys Wynne, both passed on their enthusiasm for the wild plants that grew in their County Wicklow gardens, probably never realising what long-lasting gifts they were bestowing on me.

When the flickering black-and-white screen came to live in the corner of our drawing room in the mid-1950s, we watched, with awe, stories of the Komodo Dragon and the beginning of the career of a major source of inspiration to so many: Sir David Attenborough. His enthusiasm for nature has always been like a beacon shining its light on the natural world around us, stimulating our inquisitiveness and guiding our quest for knowledge. We know how fortunate we are to have such a figure in our lives!

In the following decades, Éamon de Buitléar's programmes about our own fauna and flora educated many of us, and enlightenment came from Michael Viney's long-running column in *The Irish Times*. In recent years, Colin Stafford-Johnson has carried on the work of continuing to boost our awareness and knowledge of what surrounds us and needs our protection.

It seems an awful shame that the study of nature appears to play such a small role on the school curriculum at junior level. If young people moved into the senior cycle knowing a couple of dozen wildflowers, birds, butterflies and trees, that knowledge could be the foundation for a lifetime's engagement with the wider environment. When I was a kid in school we had a 'Nature Walk' about once every term. We were lucky.

Beech tree beside Vartry Reservoir in County Wicklow

We had one teacher who obviously had a *grá* for nature and she passed it on to some of us. One thing it taught us was the utter joy of being out in the open during school hours but it also introduced some of my classmates to a few of the elements of the world around them, which until then they had never noticed.

If I was asked what single thing I would do to attract a young person's attention to the environment, I would say: get down to his or her level and think small. Give the child a little hand lens and take them outdoors. Watch as he or she studies a ladybird or a tiny flower, up close – captivated, spellbound, absorbed. It's a small act but could be enough to inspire another Darwin.

For myself, I can only continue to try and spread the word about our precious and fragile biodiversity, how much we need to respect it and conserve it for the future. I try not to be pessimistic or negative about what is happening to our environment but it is difficult when I return to see a particular wildflower only to find that the habitat has changed and that yet another species has lost a home. All I can hope to do is to encourage people – young and old – to get out and savour what is there, trying to help them to know a little more about what is around them. Perhaps, that way, they will help to preserve it.

Acknowledgements

I would like to acknowledge the help and support of the following people:

Petra Devlin and Pete Devlin for patiently listening and reading – and their bravery in reacting honestly.

Nik Devlin for his very clear memories.

Juanita Browne for her expertise in proof-reading and her excellent suggestions.

Dr Matthew Jebb, Director, The National Botanic Gardens, Dublin for his consistent support, encouragement and help.

Paul Green for generously sharing his botanical knowledge.

Jackie O'Connell, Paula O'Meara and Christine Cassidy for helping me to find some wildflower species.

Tomas Murray and Angus Tyner for sharing their knowledge on butterflies.

Colette Farmer and Janet Whelehan for reading through certain chapters and giving me their honest feedback.

All at The Collins Press for their enthusiasm and encouragement over the last few years.

Con Nyhan, formerly with Coillte, for sharing his recollections of Glenmalure.

Gerry Daly, Editor, *The Irish Garden* for his identification of *Inula hookeri*.

Royal College of Physicians of Ireland for permission to reproduce their image of Dr Kathleen Lynn catalogue reference SU/8/3/18.

Penelope Durell for allowing me to use information from her book *Discover Dursey*.

John Eagle for information on Dursey Island's cable car.

Mike Lynch, Archivist, Kerry Library, and John Fitzgerald, Seaweed Walks, for their help with information on Deenish Island.

Ganley Walters for use of their picture of Tigroney, Avoca, County Wicklow.

Jane Powers, Charles Nelson, Katie Donovan and Margaret Donovan for their help in finding Primula 'Julius Caesar'.

Jane Maxwell, Principal Curator, Library of Trinity College Dublin, for use of the Wynne family papers with regard to Emily, Winifred and Veronica Wynne, Avoca, County Wicklow.

Dr Anita Donaghy, Senior Conservation Officer, BirdWatch Ireland, and Sam Birch, National Parks and Wildlife Service, Corncrake Fieldworker, Cleggan, for their help with regard to the distribution of the Corncrake.

Padraic Flood, Max Planck Institute for Plant Breeding Research, Germany, for help with Thale Cress.

Dundalgan Press Limited, who are, after more than 150 years, still in the printing business, for permission to reproduce the front cover of *An Irish Flora*.

Ferdia MacAnna, Brendan Nangle and Adrian Taheny for their suggestions and contributions with regard to my writing.

Members of the Dalkey Library Writers' Group for their generous feedback.

Plant Index

Note: illustrations are indicated by page numbers in **bold**.

Index

Note: illustrations are indicated by page numbers in **bold**.

Insects

Mammals

General

Also by Zoë Devlin

The Wildflowers of Ireland
A Field Guide
Discover the fascinating world of Ireland's diverse collection of native wildflowers: from the insect-eating Sundew to the humble Harebell, this illustrated guide features over 530 of the wildflowers of Ireland with more than 1,200 of the author's photographs.
ISBN 978-1848892026

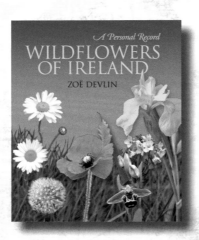

Wildflowers of Ireland
A Personal Record
Passionate about this often-overlooked part of our natural heritage, Zoë Devlin presents a personal record of the wildflowers that adorn Ireland's countryside. Her descriptions and photographs of the plants are enhanced with herbal and literary references and related Irish folklore.
ISBN 978-1848891265

Also from The Collins Press

Ireland's Wild Orchids
A Field Guide
BRENDAN SAYERS AND SUSAN SEX
Amongst the loveliest of our wild plants, orchids are found in a great variety of habitats in Ireland. This practical guide contains expert illustrations, photographs of each plant in situ and clear instructions for identification, with notes on size, habitats, flowering period, distribution and variations.
ISBN: 978-1848891692

Ireland's Trees
Myths, Legends and Folklore
NIALL MACCOITIR
ORIGINAL ILLUSTRATIONS BY GRANIA LANGRISHE
Many myths and legends and much folklore associated with native Irish trees persist to this day and they are gathered together here. Two main themes emerge: the tree as a marker of important places such as royal sites or holy wells, and the role of trees as sources of magical power in folk customs and superstitions.
ISBN: 978-1848892484

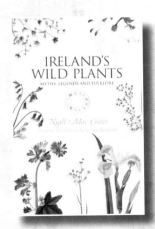

Ireland's Wild Plants
Myths, Legends and Folklore
NIALL MACCOITIR
ORIGINAL ILLUSTRATIONS BY GRANIA LANGRISHE
Ireland's wild plants have been part of our culture and folklore from the earliest times, featuring in the Brehon Laws, early Irish poetry and herbal medicine. Plants are described in seasonal order and different aspects are examined, such as their roles in charms and spells, Irish place names and folklore cures.
ISBN: 978-1848892491

Also from The Collins Press

Heritage Trees of Ireland

TEXT BY AUBREY FENNELL, IMAGES BY CARSTEN KRIEGER AND KEVIN HUTCHINSON

Trees are a precious part of Ireland's heritage, some remarkable for age or size, location or aesthetic appeal, history or folklore. Presented here are 150 trees unique to Ireland with connections dating back over thousands of years.
ISBN: 978-1848891593

Whittled Away

Ireland's Vanishing Nature

PÁDRAIC FOGARTY

Authoritatively charts how the grim failure to manage our natural resources has impoverished our country but also reveals possibilities for the future and shows how nature and livelihoods can recover hand in hand. A provocative call to arms, Whittled Away presents an alternative path that could lead to a brighter future.
ISBN: 978-1848893108

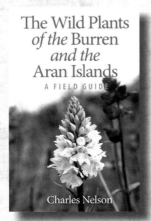

The Wild Plants of the Burren and the Aran Islands

A Field Guide

CHARLES NELSON

The Burren and the Aran Islands are renowned worldwide for their beautiful wild flowers and plants. Here are 139 of the most widely occurring plus a number of special and elusive plants, including the recently rediscovered Arctic sandwort.
ISBN: 978-1848892668